The Sur... ...appointment

Winsome. Honest. Faithful. Those are the words that come immediately to mind when I think of the writing of John Koessler. He writes with engaging charm, with frank honesty about the rough texture of life, and with a grounded faith that will not be moved. It's why I publish anything I can by him in *Christianity Today*. It's why you should read everything he writes, starting here.

—**MARK GALLI,** editor, *Christianity Today*

When you experience disappointment with people, you're human. You reach a different level when you become disappointed with yourself. But when you become disappointed with God, you've arrived at the place where grace can mend a broken heart. This is a book for anyone who has been hurt, let down, and bruised. It's for all of us.

—**CHRIS FABRY,** host of *Chris Fabry Live!* and author of *Borders of the Heart*

The Surprising Grace . . . marks yet another fresh insight from the pen of John Koessler. Tackling a universal and thorny struggle nearly everyone faces, Koessler comes at it with his remarkable ability to put the theological cookies on the lower shelf where laypeople like me can reach them. And they taste good.

—**JERRY B. JENKINS,** novelist and biographer

All of us as Christians have been disappointed by Jesus; yes, we all have to admit He has often not answered our prayers according to our liking; He has not healed the sick or given us the opportunities we had hoped for. But yes, in this book we learn that disappointments are also surprising marks of "grace." Even as Jesus displayed in the New Testament, our disappointments are His *appointments* to lead us to deeper relationship with Him. Read this book and be encouraged, then pass it along to someone who even needs it more than you did!

—**DR. ERWIN LUTZER,** senior pastor, the Moody Church

Here is a strong antidote for glib, shallow Christianity, and a helpful guide for those on the lifelong quest to understand how the Bible and life align.

—**CRAIG BRIAN LARSON,** pastor, Lake Shore Assembly of God, Chicago

In the tradition of Philip Yancey's singular book *Disappointment with God*, John Koessler's layered approach to a haunting subject reaches a variety of readers. He stirs long-resigned Christians by surprising them with unsentimental yet poignant takes on familiar truths. He prods the cynical with hard-hitting, unsparing honesty, and his fresh, thoughtful interpretations of biblical narratives instruct the layperson while inspiring teachers and pastors to look at Scripture more creatively.

It is rare to find theological truth delivered in literate prose, a consistent mark of Koessler's writing. His gifts of insight and respect for language, combined with engaging personal stories and a broad range of allusions to other writers and theologians, make this book stand out among its peers.

—**DR. ROSALIE DE ROSSET,** professor of communications and literature Moody Bible Institute

The Surprising Grace of Disappointment is both challenging and comforting in its honest and biblical interaction with the various ways in which God disappoints His people. Dr. John Koessler helps us to see the danger of our own agendas and expectations when we are not rooted in the sovereign purpose and plan of the God who knows and loves His people. This is a book that will steer the reader away from a demanding presumption and toward an expectant fiath that really believes that God's ways are not our ways, and that this is a good thing. His ways are better.

—**JOE THORN,** author, *Note to Self: The Discipline of Preaching to Yourself*; Lead Pastor, Redeemer Fellowship, St. Charles, IL

The Surprising Grace of Disappointment

FINDING HOPE WHEN GOD
SEEMS TO FAIL US

John Koessler

MOODY PUBLISHERS
CHICAGO

Some of the chapters in this book are developed from articles appearing in *Christianity Today* or PreachingToday.com. Chapter 1 is based on "Disappointed with Intimacy," *Christianity Today*, November 2011; chapter 3 on "Jesus Disappoints Everyone," *Christianity Today*, April 2011; chapter 4 on "Back to Reality," PreachingToday.com; chapter 5 on "Asleep at the Wheel," PreachingToday.com; and chapter 7 on "Eat, Drink, and Be Hungry," *Christianity Today*, August 2007. Parts of chapter 9 appeared in "The Hallelujah Chorus," PreachingToday.com and "The Trajectory of Worship," *Christianity Today*, March 2011.

Published in association with the literary agency of Mark Sweeney and Associates, Bonita, Florida.

Edited by Ed Gilbreath
Interior design: Smartt Guys design
Cover design: John Hamilton Design
Cover image: iStock "Closed" sign: Claran Griffin

LIBRARY OF CONGRESS CATALOGING-IN-PUBLICATION DATA
Koessler, John
 The surprising grace of disappointment : finding hope when God seems to fail us / John Koessler.
   pages cm
Includes bibliographical references.
ISBN 978-0-8024-1056-6
1. Consolation. 2. Disappointment--Religious aspects--Christianity. I. Title.
BV4905.3.K63 2013
248.8'6--dc23

2013002547

We hope you enjoy this book from Moody Publishers. Our goal is to provide high-quality, thought-provoking books and products that connect truth to your real needs and challenges. For more information on other books and products written and produced from a biblical perspective, go to www.moodypublishers.com or write to:

Moody Publishers
820 N. LaSalle Boulevard
Chicago, IL 60610

1 3 5 7 9 10 8 6 4 2

Printed in the United States of America

For Ron and Margaret Moss—
dear friends and faithful followers of Christ

Contents

Foreword

Every child enters the world crying.

Disappointment is non-optional equipment. A wise observer said many centuries ago that human beings are born to suffer just as sparks fly upward.

Sometimes, disappointment comes to thwart foolish wishes and immature dreams that richly deserve oblivion. I'm deeply grateful my earliest prayers were not answered. One of my first desires was to grow up to be Popeye the Sailor Man; and I am glad for a hundred reasons that did not happen—only one of which is that Olive Oyl turned out to be much less attractive to me when I became a man than she was when I was seven.

But sometimes disappointment comes to good hopes and wonderful desires. Somebody has a deeper hunger for a strong, rich, life-affirming marriage. Somebody hopes to have an education and pursue wonderful knowledge, but they grow up in poverty and never have the opportunity. Somebody hopes to be reconciled with an impossible parent. Somebody hopes that their child won't die.

Then comes disappointment.

There is much about the subject that I will never understand.

It cannot be explained glibly; and attempts to do so cause more harm than good.

And yet . . .

No human being can grow into the right person without it. Dietrich Bonhoeffer wrote that no one is safe for a community if they have not first been dis-illusioned; if they have not died to their illusions about a community of perfect people, and been awakened through that disappointment to their call to love the actual people that God places around them.

In a recent time of personal disappointment, I read these words written centuries ago by a spiritual guide named Francois Fenelon (in *The Royal Way of the Cross*):

God must tear from us what we love wrongly, unreasonably, or excessively, that which hinders his love. In so doing, he causes us to cry out like a child from whom one takes the knife with which it would maim or kill itself. We cry loudly in our despair, and murmur against God, as the petulant babe against its mother; but he lets us cry, *and saves us nevertheless!*

Disappointment is where dreams go to die.

The Bible is a story of disappointment. For Israel, the greatest disappointment was called the exile. In exile the people of Israel lost all their spiritual props—lost the temple, lost Jerusalem, lost the sacrificial system, lost pilgrimages, lost their sacred calendar— they lost all the indicators that told them God was present.

Yet they found this strange and costly truth—God is sometimes present to us in disappointment in ways that He is present in no other times, for in disappointment we know that God is all we really ever have.

For the Bible is not first of all the story of human disappointment. It is, in a strange way, the story of the disappointment of God. We appointed other idols in His place, and He was "dis-appointed" by the human race.

And yet this very dis-appointment, which was fully expressed on the cross where a rejected Messiah was executed, became the ultimate triumph of grace.

In these pages, John Koessler walks through the strange intersection of disappointment and grace. He walks through the journey both in Scripture and in everyday life. I hope in these pages, as in moments of disappointment, grace is the surprising message playing just beneath the surface.

JOHN ORTBERG
Author of *The Life You've Always Wanted*
Senior Pastor, Menlo Park Presbyterian Church, Menlo Park, California

At the Intersection of Expectation and Disappointment

I once had a friend who spoke with Jesus in her dreams. He showed up unexpectedly, like a friend who drops by on a whim. When I asked her what Jesus said to her on these occasions, she just smiled and shook her head, as if that explained everything. "That's my Jesus!" she said.

I suppose I should have been happy for her. But I wasn't. I was jealous. Although this sort of thing didn't happen to her every night, it happened often enough to make me wonder why Jesus never appeared in my dreams.

Then one night, He did. He sat down on the edge of my bed with a grin and began to speak. He wasn't what I expected. He had the robe and the sandals. But His hair was swept back as if it had been styled with a blow-dryer. To be honest, He looked more like a blond surfer dude from California than the Jesus I read about in the Gospels. And He wasn't making any sense. The longer He spoke, the more I realized that what He was saying was gibberish.

That's when I woke up. I had longed for an intimate encounter with Jesus like my friend's. Instead, I met His Hollywood stand-in. That was forty years ago, in the early days of my Christian experience.

Since then I have discovered that there is more to the Jesus of the Gospels than the Jesus of my dreams. The Jesus we meet in Scripture is more astonishing than anyone we could ever have imagined. He is enigmatic and reassuring. He is a comfort and a terror. He is a puzzle to His friends and an outrage to His enemies. The Jesus of Scripture says and does the most outrageous things. He does not resemble the simpering Jesus of Hollywood or the nagging Christ I often hear about in church. He is the most interesting person I have ever encountered. He is not at all what I expected.

The same is true of my Christian experience. I used to believe that the cup of grace was a draught without bitterness. What I once expected from my Christian life is best summed up by the old worship chorus we used to sing that began, "Every day with Jesus is sweeter than the day before." Since then I have learned that the truth is more complicated. Some days are sweeter than others. Some are not sweet at all. Some days are just dull, and a few are more like a nightmare than a dream come true.

Over the years I have noticed that the church has two basic approaches for dealing with this discrepancy between expectation and experience. One approach is to assure us that we are mistaken. Things are not as bad as they seem. God is just waiting in the wings ready to do something wonderful. All we need to do is ask Him and He will fix everything. Should that fail to happen, the problem is with us. Like Peter Pan urging the audience to will Tinker Bell back to life, we are told that we just need to believe harder and everything will work out. The other approach is more like the Marines. This line of reasoning basically says, "Life is hard, suck it up and get over it." I do not find either approach especially helpful.

In this book I have tried to avoid Tinker Bell theology and honestly face the reality of disappointment in the Christian life. Nearly every Christian I know is disappointed about something. Some of the most serious Christians are the most disappointed. How do we explain this? At the same time, my message is not "suck it up and lower your expectations." If anything, I am saying the opposite. I think you should *raise* your expectations.

The point of this book is that you can expect to meet Jesus in the most unlikely place—at the intersection of Expectation and Disappointment. The Jesus you meet there is not the Jesus of your dreams. Nor is He the airbrushed Christ of popular Christianity. He is the enigmatic and unpredictable Jesus of the Bible. You will not forget Him.

1

False Hope and Unreasonable Expectations

When Jesus Feels Too Far Away

Where can I go from your Spirit? Where can I flee from your presence?

— PSALM 139:7

My first major purchase was a submarine. I saw it on the back of a cereal box, which boasted of its prowess as a "real" diving submarine. The power of baking powder and this little vessel promised to make me master of the seas—or at least master of the bathtub. I had to have it, even though it cost me several weeks of my allowance.

The day it came in the mail, I carried it into the bathroom. Feeling the heart-pounding thrill that comes with a new purchase, I turned on the faucet. I tore open the box and realized that the submarine was smaller than I had imagined. No matter. I let the water run until it had nearly reached the top of the tub, loaded the special compartment at the bottom of the sub with baking soda, and launched it.

The sub went straight to the bottom. It did not dive. It sank.

Bubbles rose to the surface as the baking soda began to dissolve and then suddenly it bobbed back up to the surface. After a while it sank again. There was a kind of novelty in this but overall it was less than I had hoped for. A wave of disappointment washed over me and I realized that I had wasted my savings on a cheap plastic toy.

When I grew older I put such childish concerns behind me. But disappointment would not be put off so easily. Instead, it adapted to my changing tastes, attaching itself to the more complex toys of adulthood and insinuating itself into my vocation and my most cherished relationships. As a young pastor fresh out of seminary, I dove into my new job with all the hope and excitement I felt upon opening my new submarine. But it did not take long for me to realize that my lofty expectations as the shepherd of my own flock did not always match the mundane needs of my rural congregation.

Early in my tenure, when I attempted to present my long-term goals for worship, fellowship, evangelism, and discipleship to the elders, I expected them to be impressed. Instead, they looked at one another quizzically until someone finally said, "For the life of me, I can't understand why you put evangelism on this list." Well, at least I had my sermons. From the start, I felt most comfortable in the study and the pulpit. That is until one parishioner offered me advice for improving my messages. "If you can't say it in twenty minutes, it doesn't need to be said," he told me as he shook my hand after the sermon.

My work, even though it was ministry, often seemed like toil. People I loved did not always love me back. I occasionally took those who did love me for granted or treated them unkindly. I set out to make something of myself and glorify God in the process. Yet after making every effort to "expect great things from God and attempt great things for God," my accomplishments failed to reach the trajectory I expected.

Christianity without Scars

I should not have been surprised. We live in an age of unreasonable expectations. Ours is a world where promises are cheaply made, easily broken and where hyperbole is the *lingua franca*. Advertisers tell us that a different shampoo will make us more attractive to the opposite sex. Alcohol will lubricate our relationships. Purchasing the right car will be a gateway to adventure. These pitchmen promise to do far more than enhance our lives. They are peddling ultimate fulfillment.

"The problem with advertising isn't that it creates artificial needs, but that it exploits our very real and human desires," media critic Jean Kilbourne observes. "We are not stupid: we know that buying a certain brand of cereal won't bring us one inch closer to that goal. But we are surrounded by advertising that yokes our needs with products and promises us that *things* will deliver what in fact they never can."[1] Kilbourne notes that ads also have a tendency to promote narcissism while portraying our lives as dull and ordinary. They trade on natural desires but in a way that heightens our dissatisfaction and creates unrealistic expectations.

The church is not immune from this way of thinking. American popular theology combines the innate optimism of humanism with the work ethic of Pelagianism, resulting in a toxic brew of narcissistic spirituality that is pragmatic and insipidly positive. This is Christianity without scars. One in which all the sharp edges of our experience have been smoothed over. It offers a vision of what it means to follow Jesus, one that substitutes nostalgia in place of hard facts and replaces Jonathan Edwards's notion of "religious affections" with cheap sentimentalism.

Such a view has more in common with positive thinking than with those who saw God's promises and welcomed them from a distance (Heb. 11:13). It depicts a world in which "not a shadow can rise, not a cloud in the skies, but his smile quickly drives it away" (as the words to the old hymn "Trust and Obey" say). There is no place on such a landscape for someone like Job, whose path has been blocked by God and whose experience is shrouded in darkness (Job 19:8). It has no vocabulary adequate enough to express Jeremiah's complaint that he has been deceived and brutalized by God's purpose (Jer. 20:7).

Brochures for Christian conferences claim that those who attend will "never be the same." Church signs boast of being the "friendliest" church in town. In other contexts we would have no trouble recognizing such claims for what they are—the hyperbolic white noise of marketing. But when extravagant claims like these are taken up by the church, they are invested with an aura of divine authority. This is especially true when the language of biblical promise is pressed into service to support such claims.

. . .

The church cheapens Jesus' promises when it resorts to clichés and the rhetoric of spiritual marketing to describe its experience and its ministries.

. . .

In the Scriptures, Jesus sometimes employs hyperbole. He also makes bold claims for Himself and for the gospel that are not hyperbolic. The difference between His claims and those we often hear in the church is that Jesus' claims, while extreme, are not extravagant. The church cheapens these promises when it resorts to clichés and the rhetoric of spiritual marketing to describe its experience and its ministries.

The Language of Unsustainable Intimacy

One example of this is the language we commonly use to describe our relationships. In his book *The Search to Belong*, Joseph R. Myers uses the categories of physical space coined by anthropologist Edward T. Hall to describe levels of belonging in the church. Hall identified four kinds of space that define human interactions: public, social, personal, and intimate. According to Myers, the church commonly uses the language of intimacy to describe relationships which are at best close friendships. "The problem is that when I define my personal relationships as *intimate*," Myers explains, "I dilute the meaning of those relationships I hold in truly intimate space."[2]

Like the false promise of advertising, such labels exploit our natural desire for human intimacy and set us up for inevitable disappointment. It places an unreasonable burden on the small group, Sunday school, or worship service that is described this way. In reality, those contexts and relationships that can genuinely be described as "intimate" are few. Myers offers a needed reality check when he wonders whether we even want all our relationships to be intimate: "Think of all the relationships in your life, from bank teller to sister to coworker to spouse. Could we even adequately sustain all these relationships if they were intimate?"[3]

The same is true when it comes to the language the church uses to characterize the kind of relationship we can expect to have with Jesus Christ. Not long ago a former student of mine complained about the way youth leaders use what he called "the language of unsustainable intimacy" to describe our relationship with Jesus Christ.[4] "It's the sort of thing you hear when youth group leaders tell their students to 'date' Jesus," he explained. When the church uses the language of unsustainable intimacy to describe our experience with Christ, it substitutes cheap intimacy for the real thing and fails to do justice to divine transcendence.

We are like God, but God is different from us (Num. 23:19; Isa. 55:8–9). God is like us and yet He is not like us. "God is both further from us, and nearer to us, than any other being," C. S. Lewis observes.[5] We were made in God's image (Gen. 1:26). We are like Him, but He is not like us. "He makes, we are made: He is original: we derivative. But at the same time, and for the same reason, the intimacy between God and even the meanest creature is closer than any that creatures can attain with one another."[6]

Likewise, the Bible also affirms that in the Incarnation God the Son was "made like" us (Heb. 2:17). He was tempted in all things just like we are (Heb. 4:15). This commonality guarantees that we can look to Christ to find sympathy and help in temptation and opens the way for real relationship. However, the risen Christ is also a transcendent Christ. In his post-resurrection appearances, Jesus invited His disciples to "touch and see" that He was not a ghost (Luke 24:39; John 20:27). This was solid proof that the reality of Christ's humanity continued after the resurrection. But it is equally clear from these appearances that the way those disciples related to Jesus changed radically after the resurrection. Mary was told not to cling to Jesus' physical form because He must ascend to the Father (John 20:17). The same John who speaks so familiarly of seeing and touching Christ and who laid his head on the Savior's breast falls at Jesus' feet as one dead (Rev. 1:17).

Just as Jesus' disciples did not relate to Christ the same way after the resurrection as they did prior to this event, our relationship with Jesus is not with Christ as we find Him in the Gospels. We worship an ascended and glorified Christ. In the resurrection, the veil that hid Christ's divine glory from view was torn away. Jesus is still like us but He is also unlike us. We will be glorified "like Him" but in a day that is still to come (1 John 3:2).

According to Jesus, no one knows the Son except the Father and no one knows the Father except the Son "and those to whom the Son chooses to reveal Him" (Matt. 11:27). This is a

. . .

Christian mystics warned that in our experience with Christ we should expect desolation, pain, and suffering.

. . .

revelation of the Father "without which every eye is dark, and by which any eye that He wills may be enlightened."[7] But it is not an ordinary relationship. We do not interact with the Father the way we interact with a parent, sister, or lover. It is true that Christian mystics like the sixteenth-century Spanish nun Teresa of Ávila have long used the language of intimacy to describe their experience of Christ. Teresa spoke of Christ as both a friend and a lover. But she also warned that in our experience with Christ we should expect desolation, pain, and suffering.

Why We Can't Sense God's Presence

The Bible uses images of intimacy to characterize our relationship with Christ. We are compared to a bridegroom and bride, husband and wife, and a parent and child (Isa. 54:5; Rev. 21:2, 9; Matt. 7:11). The difference between these and the "language of unsustainable intimacy" is that the language we often use gives the false impression that intimacy with Christ can be experienced and maintained by the same mechanisms that sustain ordinary relationships: physical presence, touch, and conversation. Presence is an important element in our relationship with Christ. Jesus promised to be with us "until the end of the age" (Matt. 28:20). But this is a spiritual and invisible presence that is mediated through the Holy

Spirit rather than a physical presence. John could say that he had seen and touched Christ, but we cannot (1 John 1:1). Our peculiar blessing is to be in intimate fellowship with One who is invisible to us (John 20:29). We are in a similar position when it comes to prayer. It is true that we enjoy a kind of conversation with Jesus through the exercise of prayer, but it often feels like a one-sided conversation. He responds to our prayers but remains audibly silent. What was said of the Jews with regard to the Father could be said of us with respect to Christ: "You have never heard his voice nor seen his form" (John 5:37).

There is a kind of hearing in our relationship with Christ. Jesus said, "My sheep listen to my voice; I know them, and they follow me" (John 10:27). But for most, this hearing is not audible. Jesus does speak through Scriptures, but this is communication by means of inference. We extrapolate what Christ is saying to us through something that was either spoken or written to someone else. This is not like ordinary conversation.

God, of course, is never truly absent. There is no place that we can go to escape His presence (Ps. 139:7–12). But the fact that He is everywhere and always present does not guarantee that we will sense His presence. To the contrary, absence is as much a fact of our experience of God as the reality of His presence.

Why is this so? One reason God seems to be absent is because of sin's intrusion into divine and human relationships. According to Genesis 3:7–8, as soon as Adam and Eve became aware of God "walking in the garden in the cool of the day" after they had eaten from the forbidden tree, their first instinct was to hide "among the trees of the garden." It is not God who prefers to keep a distance but us. Our relationship with God and with one another was not entirely destroyed by sin, but it was distorted. We do not sense

God's presence because we are trapped in a compound of our own making, hiding from God and from one another behind walls of alienation (Col. 1:21; Titus 3:3).

However, sin is not the only reason we find it difficult to sense God's presence. Absence is a normal feature of all relationships. The late Anthony Bloom wrote: "The fact that God can make Himself present or can leave us with the sense of His absence is part of a live and real relationship."[8] Bloom noted that a mechanical approach, where we try to compel God to manifest His presence simply by drawing near, has more in common with idol worship than Christian spirituality: "We can do that with an image, with the imagination, or with the various idols we put in front of us instead of God; we can do nothing of the sort with the living God, any more than we can do it with a living person."[9]

If there is an analog in our ordinary experience to the kind of mechanical spirituality Bloom condemned, it is to be found in pornography. Think about it. One appeal of pornography is that it offers sensuality without responsibility. The one who uses an image to stimulate lust craves an experience which simulates intimacy but without the obligations that comes with a real relationship. There is sensation and gratification but no mutuality. We treat God in a similar fashion when we turn to the mechanics of the spiritual disciplines hoping that they will generate a sense of His presence.

What Kind of Personality Did Jesus Have?

In Evangelicalism we often speak of our "personal" relationship with Jesus Christ. Yet we really know very little about Christ's personality. We know that Jesus possessed a personality. But we know virtually nothing about those aspects that would have made His personality distinct from that of another. We do not know anything about His appearance, and next to nothing about the sound of His voice. We know that He was a carpenter, but we do not know what He liked to do in His spare time. We know that Jesus cried but do not know what made Him laugh—or even *if* He laughed. We cannot see the gleam in His eye or the way His forehead might have wrinkled when He thought deeply about something. Indeed, we have a much clearer notion of Simon Peter's personality than we do of Christ's.

Some try to resolve this dilemma by suggesting that Jesus had a perfectly balanced personality. They say that if Jesus had taken the Myers-Briggs Personality Inventory, He would have scored equally in every area. But isn't this just a way of saying that Jesus had no personality at all? What is more, if Jesus was truly God in the flesh as the Bible declares, such a scenario seems extremely unlikely. If personality is the result of a combination of factors which includes both genetic makeup and experience, then as far as His human nature was concerned, Jesus must have had His own distinctive personality. Otherwise He would not have been human.

There are, of course, moments in the Bible when the clouds part and a ray of personality peeks through: Jesus looks around in anger or feels love for a young man who has rejected His call to follow (Mark 3:5; Mark 10:21). He speaks tenderly to a shy woman (Luke 8:48). Yet even in these instances we learn more about Jesus' character than we do His personality. The Bible is mostly silent on this subject. However, our ignorance of the details of Christ's human personality does not prevent us from having a personal relationship with

> • • •
>
> **Our relationship with Christ is one in which we are known more than we know.**
>
> • • •

Him. Jesus' promise to come to the disciples after His departure is proof that physical absence does not mean a lack of presence (John 14:18). The ascension of Christ paved the way for the ministry of the Holy Spirit to the church (John 16:7). The advent of the Holy Spirit makes it possible for us to experience true intimacy with Christ.

This intimacy is unlike any other relationship with which we are familiar. Our relationship with Christ is one in which we are known more than we know (1 Cor. 13:12). The comfort we find in the conversation of prayer is the comfort of being heard more than of hearing (1 John 5:14–15). It is a relationship that is personal but reveals little about Jesus' personality. It is also a relationship where our greatest intimacy is to be experienced in the future rather than the present. This means that for the present we should not expect to find ultimate fulfillment in our experience of Christ. That is yet to come. We may even find on occasion that human relationships are more vivid and immediately satisfying to us. Perhaps this is implied in the earthly analogies the Bible uses when it speaks of our relationship to God. These concrete experiences "put a face" on our spiritual relationship and help us to relate to the invisible God in a personal way.

Building on the Ruins

Ultimately the roots of our disappointment are much deeper than the language we use to frame our expectations. The seeds of disappointment are sown in the fabric of the world itself. To the ancients the heavens look like a model of symmetry, order, and proportion. However, this was merely an illusion created by distance. Closer inspection revealed a more terrifying reality. The heavens are full of dark matter as well as light. The Earth is teeming with life but the rest of the universe—at least the portion of it that we have been able to see—is barren. There is order, as the stars move in their courses each night and the cycles of seedtime and harvest, cold and heat, summer and winter, day and night continue just as God promised (Gen. 8:22). But there is also chaos and destruction.

Albert Einstein once observed that God does not throw dice. Yet it often seems as if the universe does. Our treatment at the hands of creation frequently feels arbitrary and at times even cruel. When tremors deep beneath the Pacific Ocean sent 124-foot waves crashing against the Japanese coast in March 2011, they triggered a chain of disasters that killed thousands and displaced more than 280,000 people. Months later the worst tornadoes in a hundred years tore through the Alabama countryside, leaving bloody scars on the landscape. In October 2012, the United States held its breath as superstorm Sandy, downgraded from a hurricane, still wiped out entire sections of New York and New Jersey, leaving communities devastated, families homeless, children dead. Jesus said that the Father causes His sun to rise on the evil and the good, and sends rain on the righteous and the unrighteous (Matt. 5:45). Tragedies like these are equally indiscriminate. They afflict both the evil and the good.

Jesus' words beg the question, if the Father is responsible for causing the sun to shine and rain to fall, who is responsible for the tsunami and the tornado and the hurricane?

Disasters of both the natural and the man-made variety are not foreign to the Bible. The great flood, Sodom's destruction, the fall of Jerusalem, and the collapse of the tower of Siloam are just a few that come to mind. It is not without cause that this kind of devastation is often described as being of "biblical proportion."

The Scriptures explain such suffering with God's larger plan in view. Jesus warned His disciples, "Nation will rise against nation, and kingdom against kingdom. There will be earthquakes in various places, and famines. These are the beginning of birth pains" (Mark 13:8).

These are not glib words. Not when they are spoken by one who wept over the destruction of Jerusalem and who willingly bared His back to the scourge "for us and for our salvation." They are not glib but neither are they comforting. They were not meant to be. They were intended to be words of warning. They are Jesus' solemn assurance that things will get worse before they get better. These things "must happen," but the end is not yet (Mark 13:7).

The collateral damage of sin—and the Bible teaches that the natural world writhes in the throes of sin's effects as much as the human soul does—cannot be avoided. Creation has been "subjected to frustration" and is in "bondage to decay" (Rom. 8:20–21). The ground that once yielded its fruit willingly now does so only after a struggle and all who come after Adam have learned to eat the bread of sorrow like their first father. The full cup must be drunk, even to the dregs. Redemption is coming. The day draws near when the Earth's groaning will cease and creation will be liberated from its bondage to decay and brought into the glorious freedom of the children of God. But that day is not today. Today we must live amidst the wreckage of the fall and build upon the ruins.

Worship Among the Ruins

The other day during my ride home from work I saw a church sign that read "Greater Works Ministries." I immediately recognized the allusion to Jesus' promise in John 14:12: "I tell you the truth, anyone who has faith in me will do what I have been doing. He will do even greater things than these, because I am going to the Father." It was not the usage of this Scripture phrase that caught my attention so much as the poor condition of the church sign. The lettering was cracked and faded, like the worn building upon which it was emblazoned. *"You would think a church that could do 'greater works' could put up a better sign,"* I mused.

. . .

The construction of the spiritual life requires as much tearing down as building up.

. . .

But there is no real incongruity between the sign's bold promise and the drab reality of its setting. If anything, the inherent contradiction implied in this visual image is a more accurate reflection of what most people experience when it comes to church than the overheated rhetoric that we use to describe it. But what are we to make of the wreckage we see around us? Is it symptomatic of our crumbling façade or proof that we are being rebuilt from the rubble? Perhaps it is both.

The construction of the spiritual life requires as much tearing down as there is building up. Sometimes the demolition is a result of God's renovating work through the Holy Spirit. We "put off" in order to "put on" (Eph. 4:22, 25). At other times it is a result of our own self-destructive behavior. Not everyone who builds the church does so carefully or with the best material (1 Cor. 3:11–13).

What we can be sure of is that despite our worst effort (and sometimes despite our best) Christ will finish the work that He has begun. He will build His church. The powers of hell will not overcome it (Matt. 16:18).

Near the end of the war with Germany, as Allied bombs rained down on Stuttgart and the Nazi regime writhed in its final death throes, Lutheran pastor and theologian Helmut Thielicke preached a remarkable series of sermons on the Lord's Prayer to his church. With the battered remnant of his congregation gathered for worship in the midst of their ruined church, Thielicke used Christ's words to trace a stunning map of spiritual reality. He located their experience at the intersection of two lines of activity.

"The first line is a descending one," Thielicke preached, "and it indicates that mankind is constantly living farther and farther away from God."[10] The other line is the ascending line of Christ's dominion over our lives, which goes on simultaneously within the other process. Employing Luther's language of Christ's presence in the Sacraments, Thielicke declared: "In, with, and under the world's anguish and distress, in, with, and under the hail of bombs and mass murders, God is building his kingdom."[11]

This is not hyperbole. It is not pastoral spin or church marketing. It is the language of spiritual reality.

2

As Good as His Word

When Jesus Is Not Who We Thought He Was

They got up, drove him out of the town, and took him to the brow of the hill on which the town was built, in order to throw him down the cliff.

—*LUKE 4:29*

Months before Jesus returned to Nazareth, stories about Him echoed through the hills of Galilee like the thunder of an approaching storm. From the highlands of Cana, where something happened to the wine at a wedding, to the big town of Capernaum on the shores of the Sea of Galilee, strange reports about His doings trickled back to His hometown. People said that He was more than a preacher. They claimed He was a prophet. Some said He was a miracle worker, maybe even the Messiah.

If Jesus did not arrive in Nazareth unannounced, neither did He come as a stranger. Jesus grew up there. He worshiped in its synagogue and played in its streets. Jesus learned the carpenter's trade at Joseph's side while living in Nazareth. No doubt there was a time when the village mothers speculated about which of their daughters He would eventually marry. But that was before Jesus took to the road, forsaking the carpenter's trade for a life of poverty as an itinerant preacher.

Now, according to Luke 4:14–28, Jesus had come home, at least for the moment. Despite the rumors about Him, He did not look much different than when He left. He certainly did not look like anyone's idea of a prophet, much less like the Messiah. Although some thought He bore a family resemblance to John, who had suddenly appeared in the desert baptizing and preaching as if out of nowhere, Jesus lacked the Baptist's stark appearance and austere manner. John came in camel's hair crying repentance. Jesus preached repentance, too. But to the people of Nazareth, He looked like a carpenter. That is to say, He looked like Jesus, the familiar son of Mary and Joseph. They knew His brothers James, Joseph, Simon, and Judas. They knew His sisters, who still lived in Nazareth. They knew Jesus. Or at least they thought they knew Him.

On that Sabbath Jesus took His usual place in the synagogue, just as He had done many times before. As expected, the president of the assembly invited Jesus to read from the Scriptures, a courtesy acknowledging His new status as a popular rabbi. He handed Him the scroll of the prophet Isaiah and Jesus unrolled it, searching until He found the spot He wanted. Then He began to read:

> The Spirit of the Lord is on me,
> because he has anointed me
> to preach good news to the poor.
> He has sent me to proclaim freedom for the prisoners
> and recovery of sight for the blind,
> to release the oppressed,
> to proclaim the year of the Lord's favor (4:18–19; see Is. 61:1–2a)

Jesus handed the scroll back to the attendant and sat down—a signal that He was about to teach. What followed was one of the shortest messages the congregation had ever heard. Jesus' "sermon" consisted of a single sentence: "Today this Scripture is fulfilled in your hearing." The congregation marveled at first, astonished by the gracious promise implied in Jesus' claim. Then someone cried indignantly, "Isn't this Joseph's son?" Like a prodigal wind that runs before an unexpected storm, the question heralded a sudden change in mood. Sensing the shift, Jesus gave voice to the challenge implied in the question.

• • •

If Jesus really did have the power that others said, was it too much to ask Him to prove it by healing His own in Nazareth?

• • •

"Surely you will quote this proverb to me: 'Physician, heal yourself!'" He said. "'Do here in your hometown what we have heard that you did in Capernaum'" (v. 23).

Was this so unreasonable? If Jesus had healed in Capernaum, why not heal in Nazareth? Nazareth had its own sick and its own crippled. If Jesus really did have the power that others said, was it too much to ask Him to prove it by healing His own? After all, the carpenter's son had just made the audacious claim that He was the Lord's anointed, the one whose coming was to signal the age of salvation. Yet instead of conceding to the difficulty of their position, Jesus' reply sounded more like a condemnation.

"I tell you the truth," He told them, "no prophet is accepted in his hometown. I assure you that there were many widows in Israel in Elijah's time, when the sky was shut for three and a half years and there was a severe famine throughout the land."

Any Jew who knew his history would see Jesus' point. Zarephath was a Gentile town on the coast between Tyre and Sidon. God sent Elijah there to take refuge in the house of a widow and provided miraculously for them both (1 Kings 17:8–16). As if He had not made His point clear enough, Jesus continued with another example from Elijah's successor, pointing out that although there were many in Israel with leprosy in the time of Elisha the prophet, the only one who was cleansed was Naaman the Syrian.

To any who might have considered themselves superior to the rabble that Jesus had taken up with in Capernaum, this was like offering someone the kiss of greeting and getting a slap in return. The mood of the crowd turned ugly. They drove Jesus from the synagogue and dragged Him to a nearby cliff intending to throw Him off. Instead, Jesus walked through the crowd. With His back to the mob, He made His way toward the path that leads out of town like a man taking a walk on a spring day.

One can easily imagine the crowd arguing amongst themselves about what had happened after Jesus disappeared from view. Had Jesus simply stared them down? Or was it the miracle they had demanded of Him? Perhaps God struck them blind, like the prophet Elijah did when he passed through the horses and chariots of Aram at Dothan. Some may even have called it sorcery, saying that it was a trick of the devil like all His miracles.

Is It So Much to Ask?

How do we explain this encounter? How did something that started out so well end so badly? Instead of giving Him the hero's welcome He deserved, Jesus' homecoming turned into an attempted lynching. The change in disposition exhibited by His own toward Jesus is as sudden as it is shocking. One minute they are complimenting Him, thinking sentimentally about the years Jesus spent among them growing up, and the next they want to push Him over a cliff. There is no middle ground here. There is nothing luke-warm. It is feast or famine, blessing or cursing.

We might attribute this change to the mob mentality. The trouble with the mob is that they are too easily swayed. They cannot be trusted. One minute they join their voices in a rousing chorus of "He's a jolly good fellow" and give you three cheers. The next minute, without warning, they turn on you. Instead of praise they offer you the boot. They can be happy with you one minute and ugly the next.

. . .

If we are honest, even the most spiritual of us will admit that there have been times when Jesus hasn't treated us as we expected.

. . .

We see this sort of thing in politics all the time. Yesterday's hero is today's goat. Today's leader is tomorrow's loser. That's the mob mentality. If you have ever been in leadership in any capacity, you know how quickly the crowd can turn and how unfair its assessments sometimes are. We could read this account of Nazareth's rejection of Jesus and dismiss it as the fickle whim of the crowd. We might even shake our heads as we read this story and comfort ourselves with the knowledge that we are not like them. We believe and follow Jesus. We cannot understand how such people could turn on Him so suddenly.

Yet if we look carefully at this crowd, we will find a face in it that looks uncomfortably like our own. If we are honest we must all admit that there have been times when we too have been disappointed by Jesus. If we are honest, the best of us—even the most spiritual of us—will admit that there have been times when Jesus hasn't treated us as we expected.

We asked Christ for some small thing. It was a trifle really.

Certainly nothing that would be beyond the scope of one who has the power to fling the stars into space. And yes, perhaps it was a little selfish. We asked for a promotion or perhaps a raise. Maybe all we asked was for a decent parking spot or a little sunshine on our day off. Is that too much to ask?

Or maybe it wasn't selfish at all. We prayed for protection or for healing. We prayed for somebody we loved. Perhaps we just prayed for hope or for some small demonstration of God's might to encourage us in a hard place, but all we got in return were the words of Scripture.

Good words.

Gracious words.

They were reassuring words, certainly.

We took comfort in the promises of Scripture. Yet when it was all over, it seemed to us that they were only words. Though we would be loath to admit it, we were disappointed. We had hoped for something more substantial than words. No, we do not have to look too hard to see ourselves among the crowd on that hill in Nazareth. I am not suggesting that we are angry enough to kill (though some of us, like Jonah, may be angry enough to die), only that we would like to find a way to pressure Jesus into seeing things our way. We are amazed by the speed with which Jesus' friends and neighbors turned upon Him. But what really troubles us is Jesus' refusal to act. What are we to make of His seeming impassibility? Why is He not moved by their request and so often by ours? Psalm 145:18 says, "The Lord is near to all who call on him, to all who call on him in truth" (Ps. 145:18). If this is true, then why doesn't God do something?

Not At Our Beck and Call

Jesus would agree with the psalmist. The Lord is near to all who call on Him. But the God who is near to us when we cry is not at our beck and call. God always hears us when we cry out to Him. He always responds. But the God who answers our cry does not answer to us. Part of the problem with the people of Nazareth was that they thought they had some special claim on Jesus. They were familiar with Jesus—too familiar really. They thought they knew Jesus. They were so familiar that they tempered their praise with a subtle correction: "Isn't this Joseph's son?" This question was intended to put Jesus in His place. It was their way of saying, "Now Jesus, don't overreach yourself. Remember who you are and remember who we are. Don't forget that we have known you most of your life!"

In the early days of my Christian experience, I found it difficult to share my faith with my father. A lapsed Roman Catholic who had gone through catechism and attended a parochial school, he had a hard time listening to his son tell him about his need for faith in Jesus Christ. "Don't you lecture me about religion," he would say. "I used to change your diapers!"

This mentality is reflected in the crowd's response to Jesus that day in Nazareth. They had heard stories about the wondrous things Jesus had done elsewhere. What they wanted was a little proof. After all, they had known Jesus since childhood. Their response may also have been affected by jealousy. Jesus was one of their own. If He was willing to display His power by performing great miracles in Capernaum, why should Nazareth be cheated? Nazareth may have been small but it was also Jesus' home. If anyone had a right to demand proof of Jesus' supposed powers, they figured surely it was those who had known Him the longest. They were profoundly disappointed when Jesus did not come through for them. They became enraged when all He offered to

• • •

We have no right to command much less to make demands of God. We are at His beck and call. He is not at ours.

• • •

substantiate His claim were the promises of Scripture and His own word that He was the embodiment of all Isaiah promised.

There was a high degree of expectation reflected in their response. This is especially surprising in view of Scripture's assessment in Matthew 13:58 and Mark 6:6 that the people of Nazareth lacked faith. Expectation, as important as it is when it comes to God, is not always a reflection of faith. Sometimes expectation is a sign of arrogance. There is a world of difference between a confident request and a demand. Both expect the same result, but the one who makes a request knows that the one of whom the request is made also has the legitimate right of refusal. Someone who makes a demand knows nothing of this. A demand also differs from a command, although the two are similar in tone and identical in expectation. One who commands possesses authority and the right to expect compliance. When it comes to God, we have no right to command much less to make demands of Him. We are at His beck and call. He is not at ours.

Get with the Plan

Nevertheless, we can grow irritated with Jesus when He seems unresponsive to our requests. We appreciate the encouragement of His Word, but would like something more substantial. Specifically, we want Him to get with the program—our program—and comply with the agenda we have set for Him. But the God who hears us when we cry also acts in His own time and in His own way. He is a God who makes promises. But He is also the one who determines how He will keep them. This is the chief difference between faith and presumption. Faith and presumption both expect something from God. Presumption wants to call the shots. Faith bows the knee.

This does not mean that faith is timid. Far from it. Abraham's faith in God gave him courage to speak frankly when pleading with God to spare Sodom and Gomorrah (Gen. 18:23–33). Abraham is so bold in this exchange that it sounds like a conversation one might have heard in the marketplace. However, unlike the merchant, when God is pressed for greater and greater concessions by Abraham, He does not put up a fight. Each time Abraham sets a new threshold of mercy, God yields to his request without resistance. Is this because God knows the real state of Sodom and Gomorrah? He can easily agree to spare them if He finds only ten righteous people, since He knows He will only find one and he is barely righteous. Or is something else going on in this exchange? Could it be that this was God's intent all along—to goad Abraham into pleading on behalf of Sodom and Gomorrah? When the two angels turned aside to make their way to Sodom and accomplish their terrible task the Lord remained, almost as if He were waiting for Abraham to say something that had not yet been said (Gen. 18:22).[1] Is it possible that Abraham stopped too soon? Perhaps God's patience should have motivated Abraham to ask God to spare the cities for the sake of only one righteous person.

Whether or not this was the case, it is clear that God went beyond Abraham's request. The Lord did something that must surely have been in Abraham's mind as he bargained, perhaps even the primary thing that motivated Abraham to speak to God in the first place. God spared Abraham's nephew Lot and his two daughters. He would have spared Lot's wife and his two sons-in-law too, if they had listened. But Lot's sons-in-law thought it was a joke and his wife ignored the angels' warning not to look back and was turned into a pillar of salt (Gen. 19:14, 26).

The Landscape of Faith

The lesson of Abraham is not that God is willing to haggle over our small concerns. It is that God's response (or seeming lack of response) to our requests must be understood in light of His larger plan. The backdrop for Abraham's request was a much larger landscape than even the patriarch knew. Abraham was primarily concerned about his nephew Lot and the doomed cities of Sodom and Gomorrah. But God's designs were more expansive. The Lord initiated this encounter because He had entered into a relationship with Abraham as a friend and as one who through Abraham would bless all the nations. What happened to Sodom and Gomorrah would have implications for generations to come (Gen. 18:17–19).

Likewise, Jesus orients His refusal to grant Nazareth's request within the framework of God's larger plan by pointing to other instances when God's blessing fell upon the unexpected and undeserving. Why should God squander His care on those outside the covenant? As Jesus rightly observes, there were many widows and lepers in Israel in the time of Elijah and Elisha. National unbelief may have played a role in God's decision to send His prophets to Gentiles.

Were the others simply collateral damage in the national battle between faith and doubt? Was their plight too insignificant to be taken into account? Everything we know about the God of the Bible compels us to reject such a thought. God who sees the sparrows when they fall has numbered the hairs on our head (Luke 12:6–7). The psalmist is right when he says that "the Lord is near to all who call on him in truth" (Ps. 145:18). But when He responds and how He responds is His call to make, not ours. God works according to His own plan and purpose. He may not always act according to our desire but we can be certain that He will act according to plan.

The certainty that God, even when He seems to be silent, is moving all things toward an inevitable end that will bring glory to Christ and holiness to the church, is the anchor that keeps us in place during the storm of doubt that rages. That anchor holds while we wait for our troubles to pass. Such confidence acts as the compass that redirects and reassures us in the dark night of the soul when Satan draws near to whisper that we are far beyond help and home.

Yet this truth may also be the hard rock of reality that causes our little ship of faith to flounder. Such knowledge may cause us to grow disheartened and become disillusioned with God. This is because it means that God cannot be coerced into doing what we want Him to do, not by prayer, practice, or will. Try as we might, we cannot drag Him to the brink and pressure Him into following our agenda. Acceptance of this fact is what separates biblical faith from positive thinking and superstition. It is what distinguishes Christian prayer from pagan magic.

We like to say that there is power in prayer, but that is not really accurate. The power does not lie in the act of praying but with God who answers. We think that it would strengthen our faith to see an answer—the more striking the better. Yet even if we got what we asked for, we might not believe it. We might explain it away as a coincidence. As far as God's refusal to grant what we request of Him or give us something other than what we asked, such instances say nothing about His capacity or His power. Jesus makes it clear that His refusal to grant the people of Nazareth the signs they requested in no way diminished His ability to do so. After leaving Nazareth, Jesus went down to Capernaum and performed the kinds of miracles Nazareth had demanded.

God's refusal to do what we ask of Him may not even say much about us. In an essay entitled "On the Efficacy of Prayer," the British scholar and Christian apologist C. S. Lewis observed that although there are passages in the New Testament which seem to promise an invariable granting of our prayers, that cannot be what they mean: "For in the very heart of the story we meet a glaring instance to the contrary. In Gethsemane the holiest of all petitioners prayed three times that a certain cup might pass from him. It did not. After that the idea that prayer is recommended to us as a sort of infallible gimmick may be dismissed."[2]

> *The Bible's list of those whose requests were refused by God is impressive.*

Lewis is right. We should not draw hasty conclusions about ourselves, "if our prayers are sometimes granted, beyond all hope and probability."[3] But it is equally true that we should not draw rash conclusions when they are *not*. The athlete who bows the knee after making a touchdown may be right in giving God the glory for his skill. But the fact that his team won the victory does not mean that he enjoys more favor in God's sight than the team that failed. The Bible's list of those whose requests were refused by God is impressive. The list includes Moses, Jeremiah, Paul, and Jesus. Should we be so surprised if God sometimes declines our own? His decisions are not arbitrary.

In the end it was doubt as much as it was disappointment that compelled the citizens of Nazareth to try to kill Jesus that day. They were not driven to this by a sense of desperation or even an awareness of great need that only God can meet. They were not looking for healing or deliverance. Not really. They were looking for a sign.

We are tempted to look for the same. We wonder how Jesus could say these things were fulfilled when we still see no evidence of all that the prophet promised. Where are the liberated poor? Where is the freedom promised to the prisoners? Where are the blind who have recovered their sight? "We too have heard of all that you did in Capernaum," we want to say. "What proof do you have for us?"

In essence, Jesus' answer to us is the same today as it was then. He is Himself the proof of all that has been promised. We, however, have an advantage that the people of Nazareth did not. We know what happened next. We know that He died and rose again. We know that He ascended to the Father's right hand, where He always lives to make intercession for us (Heb. 7:25). Because of this, heaven is not so far away that our voice will not carry to the ear of the Father. He is closer than we think. He is as close as the risen Savior who shed His blood for the forgiveness of sin and as certain as the One who sits at the Father's right hand and pleads on our behalf. This is the hope of the gospel and the center of our faith. It is a faith which believes that God is as good as His word. And because He is as good as His word, his Word is good enough.

3

Jesus Disappoints Everyone

When God Fails to Meet Our Expectations

When John heard in prison what Christ was doing, he sent his disciples to ask him, "Are you the one who was to come, or should we expect someone else?"

— MATTHEW 11:2-3

It was early in the fall semester. Ken and I were getting acquainted over lunch. I could tell by his incandescent grin that he was a freshman.

"I'm going to be a pastor," Ken said. "It's going to be cool!"

"What makes you so sure it's going to be 'cool'?"

I tried not to look amused.

He seemed shocked by the question. The radiant glow of his smile dimmed momentarily and he looked disturbed, as if I had muttered an unexpected indecency. But the grin quickly returned to his face and he dismissed my question with a shake of his head.

"I don't know," he said. "But it's going to be cool!"

A few years later I had lunch with him again. He was a senior by then and his enthusiasm had dampened. He had not quite reached the low ebb that Job's wife did. That is to say, he was not ready to curse God and die. But he did seem genuinely disappointed—with his college experience, his church, and I think ultimately with God.

As I listened to him talk, it was my turn to be disturbed. I thought back to our first lunch together and wondered what had happened to sour his disposition. He did not want to talk about it. He muttered something vague and recriminating about the church. He stared darkly at his plate and I tried to lighten the mood with small talk and encouragement. But it was no use. Try as I might, I could not resuscitate the rosy-cheeked freshman he had once been. I ate quickly and wished him the best. A few weeks later I watched him walk across the platform and receive his diploma, wondering whether his disposition would eventually improve.

> *If the Gospels are any indication, we might say that disappointment is a certainty.*

It might not. Those who serve Christ are as prone to disappointment as anyone else. If the Gospels are any indication, we might even say that disappointment is a certainty. Read the Gospels with all their sharp edges intact. What are they but a record of disappointment with Jesus on a grand scale?

Just ask John the Baptist.

Ill at ease in Herod's prison, John sent messengers to Jesus with a question: "Are you the one who was to come, or should we expect another?" The question comes as something of a surprise. After all, John was one of the first to publicly identify Jesus as the "one who was to come" (John 1:27). It was John who told Jesus, "I need to be baptized by you" (Matt. 3:14). John saw the Spirit of God descend upon Jesus at His baptism and heard the voice from heaven say, "This is my Son, whom I love; with him I am well pleased" (Matt. 3:17). If anyone had known the answer to this question, it would have been John.

It is possible that John had grown discouraged with the way his circumstances had turned out. Perhaps the darkness of Herod's prison had dimmed John's confidence in Jesus and His mission. But this, too, seems unlikely. John was used to a life of hardship. He dressed like a nomad and lived like a wild man of the desert, surviving on insects and honey (Matt. 3:4). Do we really believe that a prison cell could break his spirit? What is more, John would not have been surprised to find himself Herod's prisoner. He was a student of Scripture. He knew what happens to prophets. Nine times out of ten the prophet's fate is a bad one. John would hardly have been shocked by his experience.

Questionable Judgment

John's question is the kind my wife sometimes asks.

"Is there a reason you left your unwashed dishes in the sink?"

We have all heard questions like this and asked them many times ourselves.

"Do I have to do it myself?"

"Are you going to wear that tie with that jacket?"

"Do you work here?"

These are questions, but only in the technical sense of the word. They are not intended to solicit information. Not really. The answer is already implied in the question. So why do we ask them? Sometimes we ask them to make the other person feel foolish. The point made by the question is self-contradictory. More often the question is intended to provoke a response. The Bible is full of these kinds of questions. God, in particular, seems fond of them:

"Where are you?"

"Have you eaten from the tree that I commanded you not to eat from?"

"Who do people say I am?"

If the Bible is any indication, we are just as prone to ask such questions of God:

"Will not the judge of all the earth do right?"

"How long, O Lord, how long?"

"Are you the One who was to come, or should we expect another?"

Usually, like John, when we ask God such questions we are trying to make a point. We want God to see the inconsistency (from our perspective) of His position. We aim to provoke Him to action. And sometimes, we are even interested in His answer.

What is more, this is exactly the kind of question we would expect from John. It is the kind of question that John always asks.

"Who warned you to flee from the coming wrath?"

"I need to be baptized by You, and do You come to me?"

"Are You the One who was to come, or should we expect another?"

In this case it is John's way of saying, *"Jesus, You have forgotten Yourself."*

John's question signals the disappointment he felt about the report he had received of Jesus' ministry. The broad contours of John's expectation of Jesus were marked out in his warning to the religious leaders when they came to him for baptism. "You brood of vipers!" John had thundered. "Who warned you to flee from the coming wrath? Produce fruit in keeping with repentance. And do not think you can say to yourselves, 'We have Abraham as our father.' I tell you that out of these stones God can raise up children for Abraham. The ax is already at the root of the trees, and every tree that does not produce good fruit will be cut down and thrown into the fire" (Matt. 3:7–10).

According to John, Jesus had come to winnow the harvest. He would gather the grain and burn the chaff with unquenchable fire (vv. 11–12). Instead, Jesus was roaming the hills of Galilee, preaching the gospel and healing the sick. The ax had been sharpened and the fire kindled, but Jesus did not seem interested in either. This was so at odds with John's understanding of what Messiah would do that he could not help but question it. It is disappointment, not doubt, that lies behind John's question.

. . .

Good theology sometimes leads us to confuse God's reliability with predictability.

. . .

Failed expectation lies at the heart of every disappointment. We expect one thing and get something else instead. We expect beef for dinner and we get chicken. We thought we would get a refund from the IRS, but we end up owing money. The weather report promised sunshine for the weekend, but it rains instead. Disappointments like these are such a common experience in life, you would think that we would be used to them.

But things are different when it comes to God. We expect better treatment from Him. We know that people can be fickle. We know that people will let us down (though this knowledge does not make us any less disappointed when they do). God is not like that. We may not know much about theology, but at least we know this much: God is not a man that He should lie (Num. 23:19). He is unchangeable. There is no variableness or shadow of turning with him. He is *reliable*. Yet this good theology sometimes leads to bad practice. It causes us to confuse reliability with predictability. Because we think that God's mind and ours are the same, we set goals for God. We know what we want and so we put it in the mouth of

God. We let our desires govern our expectation.

Sometimes the goals we set actually turn out to be in alignment with what God intends to do. When that happens, we are greatly encouraged. We are so encouraged that we set more goals for God. But sooner or later—and probably it is sooner rather than later—what God does is so at odds with our expectation that we hardly know what to think.

We pray for healing and the patient dies.

The job that seemed so perfect for us goes to someone else.

That person who would have been the perfect life partner does not return our affection.

The resulting crisis is more than a crisis of faith. At least not in the way we usually define faith. Our difficulty is not that we have set the bar so high that we must now come to terms with God's inability to come through for us. The problem is just the opposite. We know what God can do. We believe that He can live up to our high expectations. Neither is this a matter of mere miscommunication. We are not troubled because we have misread the signals. What really bothers us is that we have misread the sender. We are deeply disturbed, not merely because God has failed to do what we wanted Him to do. Not even that He failed to do what we expected Him to do. We are haunted by the fact that God hasn't done what we know in our hearts that He *should* have done.

One night during my second year of college, I asked God to reveal His will for my life. As I prayed a plan seemed to stretch before me like a broad and shining path. I would transfer from the liberal arts college I was attending and enroll in Bible college. After graduation I would marry my girlfriend Debbie.

My wife's name is Jane.

A few weeks after I submitted my materials to the Bible college I had selected, I received a polite rejection along with a list of other schools that I might want to apply to instead. As trivial as they may seem to me now, at the time these two rejections rocked the foundation of my understanding of God. I did not question God's existence. But I did wonder about His judgment. I could not understand how He could get things so wrong.

How Long, O Lord?

Not all disappointments are equal. Most are minor and easily forgotten. Some are more serious. A few haunt us all our days. John's disappointment was the more serious kind. It was the sort of disappointment Jonah felt when he saw that the people of Nineveh were to be spared (Jonah 4:1–2). It was the disappointment of the prophet Habakkuk, who cried, "Why do you make me look at injustice? Why do you tolerate wrong?"(Hab. 1:3). It is the same disappointment you and I feel when we see injustice in the world around us. The poor get poorer; the rich get richer. Oppression and evil seem to be on every side and God, as far as we can tell, does little or nothing about it.

Since we are people of action as well as faith, we do what we can to make a difference. We take to the streets and befriend the homeless. We give our money to organizations that work for justice. We register to vote and try to change the system. Yet no matter what we do, the problems only multiply. The bad guys are winning. We keep looking to the hills for reinforcement but no cavalry appears on the horizon. All the while we are wondering whether the gospel is really making much of a difference. It saves the soul but it leaves the guilty unpunished. What good is the gospel if it allows a wicked ruler like Herod to treat God's prophet like his personal plaything? We are disappointed with God because

He allows the guilty to go unpunished.

There seem to be just as many who wrestle with the opposite problem. Theirs is the distress of Abraham, not the outrage of Jonah (Gen. 18:25). What disturbs them is the possibility that God might cast anyone into hell. The notion of hell seems cruel and barbarous to them, a relic of medieval culture. Many evangelicals, especially younger evangelicals, are not at all sure that such an idea is consistent with a God of mercy and grace. How can a God who "so loved the world" bear to watch His creatures suffer for all eternity? If He means to teach sinners a lesson, couldn't He think of a better way of doing so rather than casting them into a lake of burning sulfur?

> *Hell is the "awkward truth" of the Christian faith. It sticks in the craw, even of those who believe in it.*

Hell is the "awkward truth" of the Christian faith. It sticks in the craw, even of those who believe in it. Indeed, more of us than we would care to admit are practically universalists when it comes to this doctrine. I can count on one hand the number of sermons I've heard about hell in the last ten years. I can probably do the same for the number of times I have preached about it. I am not saying that we never mention it. But it is rarely the focal point of our message.

Maybe we shouldn't be surprised. Jesus talks about hell more than anyone else in the New Testament, yet He hardly mentions it at all. But when Jesus does talk about it, He speaks as if it were a real place that people go. That is to say, Jesus describes hell as if it were an actual location. It is a place where the "whole body" is cast (Matt. 10:28). Hell is a place where both the soul and the body suffer (we will return to this thorny subject in chapter 10). Many would prefer to think of hell as a state of mind or as a metaphor for annihilation. The kind of particular language that Jesus uses when referring to hell sounds archaic to the sophisticated ear.

Oddly enough, it is common to find both dispositions in the same person. Such a person is outraged and distressed all at the same time. They are frustrated with God for leaving the guilty unpunished and distressed at the thought that He would condemn anyone. They are like the people Jesus describes after John's messengers leave:

> To what can I compare this generation? They are like children sitting in the marketplaces and calling out to others: "We played the flute for you, and you did not dance; we sang a dirge, and you did not mourn." For John came neither eating nor drinking, and they say, "He has a demon." The Son of Man came eating and drinking, and they say, "Here is a glutton and a drunkard, a friend of tax collectors and 'sinners.'" But wisdom is proved right by her actions (Matt. 11:16–19).

When Jesus condemns John's generation with these words, He also condemns ours and offers a frank assessment of our ambivalence. What do we really want from God? Do we want justice or mercy? It would seem that we want justice without judgment and mercy without justice.

The Trouble with What We Want

Hell is not the only theme that has fallen out of favor in our day. Heaven has also fallen on hard times. We used to sing, "Heaven is a wonderful place, filled with glory and grace." But these days evangelicals are more likely to speak of the "kingdom" than of "heaven." To many the notion that heaven might be an actual place seems nearly as awkward as the thought of a literal hell. N. T.

Wright seems to be typical of such thinking when he asks what the ultimate Christian hope is and what hope there is for change, rescue, transformation, and new possibilities within the world in the present. Says Wright: "As long as we see Christian hope in terms of 'going to heaven,' of a salvation that is essentially *away from* this world, the two questions are bound to appear unrelated."[1] No, Christians today don't want to go to heaven. We want our heaven on earth and we want it now.

It is likely that these two things are linked. The church's neglect of the doctrine of hell springs from the same root that prompts us to marginalize the hope of heaven. Both are a result of being worldly minded. This is a major cause of all our disappointment with God. We are disappointed because we are primarily interested in the comforts of earthly life and troubled by earthly sorrows. We have forgotten Jesus' warning that there are other worse sorrows yet to come as well as better joys that cannot be described in earthly terms. The often quoted observation of C. S. Lewis was right. We are too easily satisfied: "We are half-hearted creatures, fooling about with drink and sex and ambition when infinite joy is offered to us, like an ignorant child who wants to go on making mud pies in a slum because he cannot imagine what is meant by the offer of a holiday at the sea."[2]

Even when we cry out for justice, often what we really want is merely a kind of spiritual egalitarianism. We want a heavenly bureaucracy that makes sure that everyone is taken care of. We do not *really* want justice. Not in the divine sense. How could we? If a blameless and upright man like Job, someone who feared God and shunned evil, withered under the faintest breath of God's justice, what makes us think that we could survive? God's justice is a furnace. We could not endure it in its unmitigated form any more than we could bear to walk on the sun. In his 1518 Heidelberg Disputation, Martin Luther described judgment as God's "alien" work, but it is we who are the real aliens. If Jesus was right when He said that no one is good except God alone, then none but God may be called just (Mark 10:18; Luke 18:19). When we cry out for justice, we do not know what we are asking for.

We cannot help this. We feel instinctively that hell is not our native country. The everlasting fire was created for the devil and his angels (Matt. 25:41). Yet neither are we native to heaven. When Nicodemus marveled at the idea of being born again, Jesus told him, "I have spoken to you of earthly things and you do not believe; how then will you believe if I speak of heavenly things? No one has ever gone into heaven except the one who came from heaven—the Son of Man" (John 3:12–13). Our inability to grasp the heavenly also makes it impossible for us to truly understand divine justice. The net result is a kind of myopia. Just as we are too quick to sell heaven short, we are too easily satisfied with our own tawdry vision of justice—one that is easily reducible to a government policy, political platform, or our own selfish interest.

I am not suggesting that we lack a sense of justice entirely. C. S. Lewis writes of what he calls "the law of human nature." This is an innate awareness that some standard of right and wrong exists. According to Lewis, it is most evident when people quarrel: "They say things like this: 'How'd you like it if anyone did the same to you?'—'That's my seat, I was there first'—'Leave him alone, he isn't doing you any harm'—'Why should you shove in first?'—'Give me a bit of your orange, I gave you a bit of mine'—'Come on, you promised.'"[3]

Lewis points out that remarks like these appeal to a standard of behavior that the one who makes them expects the other to know about. But they are also self-serving. Our innate sense of what justice should look like is skewed in our favor. It is this same myopic view that compels us to see the speck in another's eye with microscopic clarity while remaining oblivious to the plank in our own (Matt. 7:3–5).

This condition makes us vulnerable to a gospel without an edge to it—a gospel that is all comfort and no threat. In our eagerness to put ourselves at ease, we preach about God's love at the expense of His justice. Ironically, at the same time we are chiding our listeners for having too little regard for justice in their ethics and politics. However, when Jesus told us to fear the One who can destroy both soul and body in hell in Matthew 10:28, He was not referring to the devil. He was making a statement about divine authority and justice. It is true that heaven is the realm of God's dominion, but so is hell. Indeed, it is not in heaven that justice reigns supreme but in hell. That is because hell is the realm of God's unmitigated justice. The justice that rules in heaven is a justice tempered by grace. Abandon hell and you lose heaven as well. Because your hope of heaven depends upon the reality of God's justice. If hell does not exist, then there was no need for Jesus to suffer—the cross is meaningless and so is the gospel. Jesus taught His disciples to pray for the kingdom. But He also taught them to pray for mercy in the same breath (Matt. 6:10, 12).

Why Jesus Always Disappoints

Jesus' words in Matthew 11:16–19 reveal an even more disconcerting truth. They suggest that on some level Jesus disappoints everyone. Jesus is an equal opportunity disappointer. Jesus was a disappointment, not only for people like those of Nazareth, where they drove Him out of the synagogue and tried to throw Him off a cliff because He wouldn't perform miracles for them, but for people like those in Korazin and Bethsaida, where He *did* perform miracles. Jesus was a disappointment to friends and foes alike. He doesn't just disappoint John, but us as well.

Jesus' reply to John's question should be a clue to us that we have missed something. Our disappointment is mainly a problem of perception. What is most striking about Jesus' answer to John's question is that He provides no new information. John already knows everything that Jesus tells him. Even the description of Jesus' miracles was merely a reminder of what John has already been told. So how does Jesus' answer help? Jesus' reply alludes to Isaiah 35:5–6. As a student of Scripture, John would have recognized the reference, but it is the context of Isaiah's promise that would have struck home. Immediately prior to these verses, Isaiah says, "Strengthen the feeble hands, steady the knees that give way; say to those with fearful hearts, 'Be strong, do not fear; your God will come, he will come with vengeance; with divine retribution he will come to save you'" (Isa. 35:3–4).

What is Jesus' answer to John? In effect it is this: "Go back and tell John what you have seen and heard. Tell him that your God has come—that He has come with a vengeance. The blind receive sight, the lame walk, those who have leprosy are cured, the deaf hear, the dead are raised and most important of all, the gospel is preached to the poor. John, your God has come to save you" (see Matt. 11:4–5).

In other words, like John we are disappointed with Jesus because we do not see what He is *really* doing. It turns out that we have been laboring under a major misapprehension. Jesus came *for* us, but that does not mean that He came to *please* us. Jesus came for us, but He does not answer to us. Jesus came for us, but He will not subject Himself to our agenda, no matter how good that agenda might be. Instead, Jesus demands that we submit ourselves to His agenda.

Am I saying that the solution to our disappointment is to "suck it up" and "tough it out"? Is this the main message: "Life is disappointing; get over it"? No, just the opposite. Jesus' parting words to John's disciples were words of blessing as much as they were words of warning: "Blessed is the man who does not fall away on account of me" (Matt. 11:6). These were the last words that John would hear from Jesus before his death. They are Jesus' last words to us in our disappointment—no matter what the cause: "Blessed is the one who is not offended with Me."

In the face of great disappointment, we usually ask for an explanation. This is because we naively think that an explanation will make us feel better. Has it ever occurred to us that it might do the opposite? Instead, Jesus offers something far superior. Instead of an explanation, Jesus offers Himself. When it comes to disappointment, there is no other remedy. It is the nature of disappointment to match us measure for measure. As long as we hold on to it, disappointment will wrap itself around our heart like a great snake. The tighter we hold on to it, the tighter it will grip us. The only way to free ourselves is to bow the knee to Christ.

We can hold on to disappointment or we can hold on to Christ. We can place our disappointment under the power of the cross and hold on to hope. When we offer our disappointment to Christ, we really offer ourselves to Him. As long as we hold on to hope, we surrender ourselves to the grip of God's grace. John should have known. This is what the voice from heaven had said all along: "This is my Son, whom I love; with him I am well pleased" (Matt. 3:17; 17:5). Jesus disappoints everybody. Everybody except for One.

4

The Awkward Conversation of Prayer

When Our Petitions Fall Short

"O unbelieving generation," Jesus replied,

"how long shall I stay with you?"

—*MARK 9:19*

I imagine Peter, James, and John stumbling as they make their way down the mountain with Jesus. The change in elevation must have been disorienting. Moments ago, it felt as if they had been lifted up to heaven. Jesus had been transfigured before their eyes. Moses and Elijah appeared. A cloud of glory enveloped them as they heard God's voice speak (Mark 9:2–12).

But it does not take long for them to come down hard. Only as long as it takes to catch a glimpse of the crowd at the foot of the mountain—the sweaty, needy masses who always seem to be there. Even when Jesus and the disciples try to get away for a few days, somehow the crowd always knows how to find them. The religious leaders are there too, the theologians and guardians of tradition who always seem so angry and accusing when Jesus is around.

There in the center of it all, hunkered down and on the defensive, are the ragged disciples. They are embroiled in some kind of argument and not doing so well by the look of it. There is plenty of shouting and finger pointing. But it is the theologians who seem to be doing most of the talking. Questions are asked and the disciples are finding it hard to come up with the answers. When they do answer, their voices are shrill.

Suddenly someone in the back spots Jesus. With a rush of movement, the crowd rolls toward Him like a great wave. But Jesus does not acknowledge them. Instead he passes straight through, like Moses striding between the walls of water at the Red Sea, and aims for the religious leaders.

"What are you arguing with them about?" He asks.

There is momentary silence, as the religious leaders glare at Jesus and the disciples looked uneasily at one another. Finally, a tired-looking man steps forward. With drooping shoulders and a haunted gaze, he looks like someone who has had to carry a heavy burden a long way with no rest in sight.

"Teacher, I brought you my son, who is possessed by a spirit that has robbed him of speech," the man declares. "Whenever it seizes him, it throws him to the ground. He foams at the mouth, gnashes his teeth, and becomes rigid."

The man's tone is the sort you sometimes hear in the marketplace—the kind that pleads and accuses all at the same time. It is the kind of voice a customer uses when they think they have been cheated by the shopkeeper.

"I asked your disciples to drive out the spirit, but they could not."

The theologians stand with their arms folded in smug superiority and wait for Jesus to provide an explanation. The disciples flush red and look nervously at one another.

"O unbelieving generation, how long shall I stay with you? How long shall I put up with you?" Jesus scolds. Then more gently, "Bring the boy to me."

The boy is not exactly a child, but neither is he quite a man yet. Disheveled and dirty, he allows himself to be led until Jesus comes into view. Then he suddenly falls to the ground, foaming at the mouth and writhing.

Everyone takes a step back.

Everyone except Jesus and the boy's father.

The two of them stand side by side and watch the young man twitch in the dirt. When the seizure is over, the boy's body lies rigid on the ground. His eyes are vacant and his face is streaked with dust and spittle. After the body has stopped moving, Jesus begins to question the father. (Read the details in Mark 9:21–23.)

"How long has he been like this?"

Jesus sounds more like a physician diagnosing a patient than a prophet.

"From childhood," the father answers.

The father's earlier anger is gone now, replaced by desperation.

"It has often thrown him into fire or water to kill him. But if You can do anything, take pity on us and help us."

Now it is Jesus turn to reprove.

"As to your 'If you can . . .'"

He pauses and His tone softens.

". . . everything is possible for him who believes."

This is too much for the father. He turns his face to Jesus again and begins to weep openly.

"I do believe," he cries. "Help me overcome my unbelief!" (v. 24).

By now the crowd can sense that something is about to

happen. They begin to murmur as those in the back push forward, afraid that they will miss the great event.

"You deaf and mute spirit," Jesus declares, "I command you, come out of him and never enter him again."

The words split the air like a crack of thunder and the boy heaves as if in the throes of death. The father, who had prayed for years to hear his son's voice one last time before he dies, covers his ears to silence the shriek that erupts from the boy's lips.

Then, in a moment, it is over. The father weeps softly as the boy lies in the dirt, so pale and still that the crowd thinks he is dead. But he is not dead. When the boy finally opens his eyes, there is a look of comprehension and relief. He fixes his eyes on Jesus, who reaches down to take him by the hand and pulls him to his feet.

It takes the disciples awhile to ask Jesus what went wrong. In fact, it isn't until they have put the crowd behind them and gone indoors, out of range of prying eyes and listening ears, that someone gets the nerve to ask the question that has been on their minds.

"Why couldn't we drive it out?"

Jesus' answer is matter-of-fact, maybe even sympathetic.

"This kind can come out only by prayer" (Mark 9:14–29).

Why They Failed

Jesus' explanation affirms the importance and power of prayer. But it also begs an obvious question. If the disciples weren't relying on prayer to drive the demon out, what *were* they relying upon? The biblical text does not say. Perhaps they hoped force of will or personal charisma would be enough. Maybe they approached it like magic, employing a particular verbal formula. Whatever the method, Jesus makes it clear that their failure is the result of prayerlessness.

But before we draw too many harsh conclusions, we should note a subtle distinction in Jesus' reply. By saying that this "kind" can come out only by prayer, He seems to imply that there are other kinds who respond to different stimuli. When it comes to dealing with demons, one size does not fit all. It is also evident that the disciples expected to be successful. They were genuinely surprised by their own failure. What is more, they were not overreaching in this expectation. This was not a case where they foolishly attempted to do something they had previously only seen their master do. Jesus had given them authority to do this very thing (Mark 3:14–15). They had already driven out many demons (Mark 6:13). Jesus' complaint suggests that they could have been successful. Past experience was proof that they *should* have been successful.

Matthew's version of this incident provides an additional insight that Mark's Gospel does not mention. The disciples' inability was not merely a problem of methodology; it was a matter of faith. According to Matthew 17:20, when the disciples asked Jesus why they had failed, He replied: "Because you have so little faith. I tell you the truth, if you have faith as small as a mustard seed, you can say to this mountain, 'Move from here to there' and it will move. Nothing will be impossible for you."

Jesus did not speak of a complete absence of faith on the part of the disciples. Instead, he remarked on the size of their faith. Their failure was due to the "littleness" of their faith. It would not have shocked Jesus' disciples to hear Jesus say this about them. Indeed this trait was so characteristic of the disciples, that "you of little faith" almost serves as a pet name for Jesus' disciples in Matthew's Gospel (see Matt. 6:30; 8:26; 14:31; 16:8; Luke 12:28). We should hear affection in Jesus' voice when we read the phrase.

. . .

We, too, are tempted to think that faith operates by the laws of ordinary physics.

. . .

In view of their paucity of faith, we might have expected Jesus to tell them that little faith in the face of great problems calls for a greater faith. This was, in fact, what the disciples assumed (see Luke 17:5–6). We, too, are tempted to think this, assuming that faith operates by the laws of ordinary physics, where the force needed to move something must be equal to the size of the object being moved. Yet this is not the case with faith, especially when it comes to prayer. According to Jesus' parable, it is not necessary for faith to match the size of the request before God will respond. Only a little faith is needed. An infinitesimal amount is enough to see astonishing results.

The Nature of Faith

Our failure to grasp this makes it difficult to pray. We desperately try to gauge whether the amount of our faith is enough to trigger the desired response from God. This anxiety in turn lends itself to spiritual posturing. We put on a show, in the vain hope that our tone, volume, or posture will somehow convince God that we have the kind of faith that warrants an answer. We fuss over our delivery, in an effort to sound convinced.

Or we conclude that the weight God will give to our prayers is a function of the number of people we can persuade to take up our request. We approach prayer as if it were a kind of oral petition drive, hoping that the uncertainty of our own voice will be drowned out by the sound of so many others. We may mount a lobbying campaign, inviting those we regard as spiritual authorities to pray for us, convinced that their prayers will have more influence with God than ours.

Instead, Jesus proposes the opposite. He does not ask us to increase our faith. Our trouble is that we do not rely on the smallest amount of faith. God does not require great faith but only a small faith. A minuscule amount of faith is enough to move a mountain. If we are like the disciples, people of "little faith," it is likely that we already possess all the faith that is needed.

Faith, then, is not the same thing as confidence. The disciples had no lack of confidence. If anything, they were too confident, relying upon previous success instead of recognizing their own inadequacy. In this regard the desperate plea of the boy's father served both as genuine prayer and bold example. He exhibited the kind of faith that Jesus urges upon His disciples. It is a small faith, one that is cognizant of its own meager and ambivalent nature. Their cry should not have been "Out, you demon" but "Lord, we believe. Help our unbelief."

> • • •
>
> *A mere grain of faith is sufficient in prayer not because my faith is more powerful than my need, but because God is more powerful than my faith.*
>
> • • •

This is the essence of faith as the Bible defines it. Not confidence so much as dependence. Not blind dependence but justifiable dependence. Just because I depend upon someone or something does not mean that they are dependable. It is all too easy for me to put my trust in that which is untrustworthy. Faith may indeed be smaller than its object, but the effect of faith cannot be any greater than its object. A mere grain of faith is sufficient in prayer not because my faith is more powerful than my need, but because God is more powerful than my faith.

German theologian Helmut Thielicke rightly reminds us that the basic fact of faith is that "the arm of the Lord is stretched out over the earth without any help on our part."[1] Yet time and again we approach prayer thinking we must somehow muster enough strength to move God's arm to the location of our need and then bend it to suit our desire. We plead for His help and attention only to leave the place of prayer feeling like a child whose tugs have failed to capture the attention of an impassive and disinterested father. Prayer is relational faith. When we pray, we relate to God as one who listens and responds to our voice. John assures us: "This is the confidence we have in approaching God: that if we ask anything according to his will, he hears us. And if we know that he hears us—whatever we ask—we know that we have what we asked of him" (1 John 5:14-15).

The confidence John speaks of is one born of relationship. It is not so much a conviction about God's power, though that is surely assumed. This is a confidence that is grounded in the knowledge that God is listening. It is the confidence of boldness. In the realm of conversation, this kind of boldness expresses itself as frankness. John urges us to disclose ourselves to God without reservation because He has trained His attention upon us. If He did not care for us, would He listen so attentively?

When my son Drew was born, my wife Jane and I decided that he should spend his first night in our bedroom. Our decision was prompted as much by the anxiety we felt as new parents as much as it was by excitement. We wanted Drew to be near us, but we were also nervous and uncertain of what to expect. Consequently, we spent the entire night in vigilant wakefulness, immediately aware anytime our son stirred in his bassinet and responsive to his slightest whimper. Apart from the anxiety we felt, this is as good a picture of the kind of confidence that John describes as any. Prayer is not a desperate bid for God's divided attention. It is not our attempt to awaken God from slumber (Ps. 121:3–4). Prayer is a cry that reaches the ear of One who is already attentive and eager to respond.

Prayer as Awkward Conversation

Prayer is part of the daily routine of most Christians. We begin and end the day with prayer. We pray over our meals. In the life of the church, every public event, no matter how common, serves as an occasion for prayer. Eugene Peterson observes, "Most of the people we meet, inside and outside the church, think prayers are harmless but necessary starting pistols that shoot blanks and get things going."[2] As a result, most of us have acquired at least a rudimentary vocabulary for public prayer. We know how to begin by saying "our Father" and end by praying "in Jesus' name." We have learned to inflect our voice in that sonorous quaver which signals to others that we have crossed the sacred threshold and are about to approach the throne of grace. A few of us may even know how to employ the King James vernacular of "Thy," "Thou," and "Thine" for solemn effect.

Yet our private prayers often tell a different story. There we engage in a more awkward conversation with God. When it comes to asking for things, we are not always sure we know what we want from God. And when we do know what we want, it often turns out to be the wrong thing. We pray by rote using the same tired slogans and phrases without reflecting much on what we are actually saying or whether we really mean what we are saying. Like a driver who has taken the same route so often that he is no longer conscious of the journey, we arrive at the end of our prayer without knowing how we got there. We do not mean to be inattentive in prayer, yet we cannot help it. We start out determined to pray well.

But quicker than you can say "Our Father who art in Heaven," our mind begins to wander and our eyelids droop. Before long, we are dreaming that we are praying and then just dreaming. Twenty or thirty minutes later, we rub the sleep from our eyes and apologize to God for dozing off.

Perhaps we should take some small comfort in knowing that we are not alone in this. Matthew's Gospel tells how, on the night of His betrayal, Jesus asked Peter, James, and John to keep watch with Him in prayer. When Jesus returned to His disciples He found them asleep. "Could you men not keep watch with Me for one hour?" He asked (Matt. 26:40–41). How does one respond to such a question? The disciples did not even try.

What was it that made the disciples sleep when they should have prayed? Perhaps they grew bored while waiting. Maybe they slept from exhaustion. Sleep might have been a side effect of the distress they felt over their growing realization that Jesus would soon be leaving them. When Jesus discovered them asleep, He said, "The spirit is willing, but the body is weak." But if this is a criticism, it is also an observation. Despite our good intentions, prayer does not come naturally to us.

> • • •
> **The prayers of the Bible are marked by a bluntness that most of us would blush to hear in our own prayers. There is . . . lament, and at times even accusation.**
> • • •

Our greatest problem, however, is not our lack of creativity in the language we employ or even our lack of attention. It is the fundamental dishonesty that is so often a feature of our prayers. "The fact that we do not stand on street corners to perform our devotions ought not to blind us to the subtle temptation by which, even in private, we are led into theatrical insincere praying," Harry Emerson Fosdick warned. "We pray as we think we *ought* to. We ask for blessings that we feel are properly to be asked for, graces we *should* want, whether we do or not."[3]

Perhaps the best remedy for this is to practice the rigor of brutal honesty when we pray. The Bible itself provides us with a model. Biblical prayers include many of the elements we think should be a part of our conversation with God, like praise and polite request. But the prayers of the Bible are also marked by a bluntness that most of us would blush to hear in our own prayers. There is complaining, lament, and at times even accusation (Ps. 42:9; 43:2; Jer. 4:10; 20:7). We are mistaken if we think that we can impress God with our verbal posturing. Frankness is an essential element of genuine prayer. The sort of insincere praying that asks for what we ought to want rather than what we really want is really a form of spiritual denial. Honesty is always in our best interest, even when we are embarrassed by the truth of our own words.

The Silence of Prayer

Jesus' mention of the body in connection with the disciples' failure in the garden of Gethsemane is an important reminder that there is a physical dimension to prayer. Most Protestants think of prayer as a purely mental exercise. But it also makes physical demands upon us. The runner at the starting line listening for the signal to begin the race appears to be inactive. In reality, her attention is concentrated and her whole body is poised for action. This is a kind of waiting, but it is also active. Prayer's greatest demand may be that it requires that we restrain our tendency toward activism and wait for God.

While silence is usually a necessary context for prayer, it is also the element that makes prayer feel like a one-sided conversation.

We address God but hear no reply. We interpret this silence as a mark of God's impassivity. We are tempted to think that God is too busy to be bothered with us or that He is dismissive of our requests. It does not occur to us that silence is also the mark of a good listener. Indeed, God is such an attentive listener that He hears our cry before the words have been uttered (Isa. 65:24).

Neither does it occur to us that we might not like it if God did speak in response to our prayers. When Israel heard the voice of God at the foot of Sinai, they begged him to stop. "Speak to us yourself and we will listen," they pleaded with Moses. "But do not have God speak to us or we will die" (Exod. 20:19). As terrifying as the trumpet of God's voice must have been, it was the thundering implications of His Word that compelled them to beg Moses that "no further words be spoken to them" (see Heb. 12:19).

It would be wrong, however, to view prayer as a monologue. Prayer is a dialogue. But not the kind you would expect. In many of the Psalms the dialogue is provided by the psalmist, who speaks frankly to God and then addresses himself in reply. In Psalm 42, for example, the writer answers his own complaint that God has forgotten him with an admonition to self: "Why are you downcast, O my soul? Why so disturbed within me? Put your hope in God, for I will yet praise him, my Savior and my God" (Ps. 42:11).

Perhaps one reason we find prayer disappointing is because we have been waiting for God to speak when we should be talking to ourselves. We have concentrated on God but have neglected to address ourselves in response. If the Psalms are a model for prayer, then praying is not a two-way conversation, so much as it is a one-way conversation that moves in two directions. We speak to God and then to ourselves. We make our requests to God and then answer ourselves. "The main art in the matter of spiritual living is to know how to handle yourself," Martyn Lloyd-Jones observed. "You have to take yourself in hand, you have to address yourself, preach to yourself, question yourself."[4]

So, why pray when it is so hard? We pray because we *need* to pray. We

• • •

Prayer is not easy. But it is simple. It is as simple as the infant's cry or the beggar's reach.

• • •

pray, albeit poorly, because we can't help but pray. Most of all, we pray because God invites us to pray. Prayer is hard. But it is also simple. The nineteenth-century Anglican bishop J. C. Ryle wrote:

It is useless to say you do not know how to pray. Prayer is the simplest act in all religion. It is simply speaking to God. It needs neither learning, nor wisdom, nor book-knowledge to begin it. It needs nothing but heart and will. The weakest infant can cry when he is hungry. The poorest beggar can hold out his hand for alms, and does not wait to find words. The most ignorant man will find something to say to God, if he has only a mind.[5]

The old bishop was right in this. Prayer is not easy. But it *is* simple. It is as simple as the infant's cry or the beggar's reach. The power of prayer does not lie in the rigor of its method or the beauty of its vocabulary. Its strength is not in the supplicant's posture or the prayer's length. The essence of prayer is in the asking. Prayer is fundamentally an expression of our need. "Your Father knows what you need before you ask him," Jesus assures us in Matthew 6:8. He also knows what we will say before we say it (Ps. 139:4). We cannot impress Him with our language. We will not shock Him with our bluntness.

Prayer is a declaration of dependence upon the God who sustains our life. It is a moment-by-moment confession that in Him we live and move and have our being. As I get older in the Christian life, prayer doesn't seem to be getting any easier for me. But it really couldn't be simpler.

5

Asleep at the Wheel

When Jesus Is Missing During the Storm

The disciples went and woke him, saying,

"Master, Master, we're going to drown!"

—*LUKE 8:24*

One day Jesus and His disciples set out in a boat to go over to the other side of the lake. Several of Jesus' disciples were fishermen. They were professionals when it came to the water. No doubt they looked at the sky before they set out and scanned the horizon for any indicators of inclement weather, and all signs pointed to smooth sailing. Yet they soon found themselves fighting some of the toughest waters they had ever faced, wondering if they were going to make it out of the storm alive. As they sailed, "a squall came down on the lake" (Luke 8:22–23).

A squall is a little word for a big wind. In this case it was an especially big wind. It dropped from the sky like a bird of prey, swooping down on their small craft with so much velocity that they were helpless in the face of it. The storm howled like a demon and churned the sea to a boil. It was the kind of storm that can snap a mast or cause a small craft to heel over and go to the bottom. Perhaps this storm was what sailors call a "white squall," a microburst of wind but without the dark clouds that mark an ordinary storm. The squall struck the disciples' little craft with the force of a cannon.

Perhaps, if they had been able to see the storm looming on the horizon, they could have steered clear of it. But there was no warning. Since they were unable to get out of the way, they braced themselves and attempted to sail through it to the best of their ability. That's what you do in times of trouble. You try to prepare. You batten down the hatches and adjust the sails. You do the best you can. But this wind was too big. Not only were they unable to make headway, in a matter of minutes their little craft was in danger of being swamped. How long had they been fighting the storm before someone thought, "Hey, where's Jesus?" To their dismay, they realized He was just where they had left Him at the beginning of the voyage: fast asleep in the stern of the ship.

I do not think that they crept up to Him on tiptoe, shook Him gently, and whispered in His ear to wake Him. They screamed, if only to be heard over the shrieking wind. More than that, they cried out in terror.

"Master, Master, we're going to drown!" they said.

It would not surprise me if their tone was like that of the captain of the ship that the Old Testament prophet Jonah boarded in the hope that it would take him to Tarshish. As the sailors struggled on deck to keep the ship from going down, the captain found God's prophet down below. Jonah wasn't hiding. He was sleeping, resting as if he didn't have a care in the world. The captain went to him and demanded, "How can you sleep? Get up and call on your God! Maybe He will take notice of us, and we will not perish."

I don't know if the disciples thought about the captain's question as they made their way to the stern and shook Jesus awake, but they certainly shared his spirit. Their cry was shrill—its note of chiding unmistakable. "Master, how can You sleep at a time like this?" they seem to say. "Don't You know that we are all about to die? Don't You care?"

Who can blame them? The storm is raging. The boat is going down. But Jesus is a different story. There is no panic with Him. He doesn't leap to His feet with a gasp and demand to know why they didn't wake Him sooner. Instead, Jesus gets up and speaks. He rebukes not only the wind and the water but the disciples as well. "Where is your faith?" He asks.

. . .

When Jesus speaks, the wind grows quiet. But a different kind of storm has begun to brew in the disciples' hearts.

. . .

The effect on the storm is immediate. When Jesus speaks, the wind grows quiet. The churning waters still themselves like a spent child who has exhausted himself after a tantrum. But a different kind of storm has begun to brew in the disciples' hearts.

"Where is your faith?" Jesus asks, and they reply with a question of their own.

"Who is this?" they say. "He commands even the winds and the water, and they obey Him!" (Luke 8:24–25).

Two Puzzling Questions

One cannot help being struck by the counterpoint reflected in these two questions. First, there is the question posed by Jesus to the disciples: "Where is your faith?" Something inside me wants to answer back, "How can you ask such a question, Jesus? The boat was sinking!" What did Jesus expect the disciples to do? He was fast asleep when the storm struck. The danger was real. If these experienced sailors were afraid, the threat must have been genuine.

Yet any challenge I might be tempted to offer dies on my lips when I hear the question asked by the disciples. "Who is this?" they ask. "He commands even the winds and the water, and they obey Him." Why were the disciples so surprised? If they didn't think Jesus could do anything about the wind and the water, why did they wake Him? Better to let Him go to the bottom while still asleep.

These two questions chart the landscape of our spiritual lives. Like an explorer who discovers an undiscovered country and then plots it on a map, they mark the boundaries of our struggle with doubt. At one pole there is the question of Jesus: "Where is your faith?" This is not an easy question to understand let alone answer. What can Jesus mean by it? Is He merely grumpy, irritated with the disciples for disturbing His nap? This seems doubtful. It certainly does not match the picture we have of Jesus elsewhere in the Gospels. Jesus was often interrupted. He frequently put His own concerns aside in order to meet the needs of others. The Gospel writers never portray Him as impatient, selfish, or petulant.

Perhaps Jesus felt that the disciples were overreacting. We all know people who are convinced that every cloud is a thunderhead and every wind a hurricane. There are no small problems for such people. Each personal setback is a tragedy, every tiny problem a major disaster. We suspect that they weary the heavens when they pray just as they weary us with their constant worrying. This, however, does not fit the picture we find in the Scriptures. Luke 8:23 says the boat "was being swamped" and that the disciples were "in great danger." The threat was real. Jesus' disciples were not exaggerating when they worried that they might drown.

Faith and Action

Maybe when Jesus asked this question, what He really meant was, "Where is your faith in yourselves?" Could He be chiding them for not taking action? We know people like that too, those who spiritualize everything. No matter what the problem, their solution is always the same: "Let's pray about it." Like Moses at the Red Sea, they cry out to God when instead they should take the next step (Exod. 14:15). There are some situations where the most spiritual response is to take sensible action. Was this Jesus' intent? Perhaps He was simply trying to urge the disciples not to stand there crying about the wind and the waves, when they already possessed the skills to address the problem at hand. Tend to the sails! Man the oars! Start bailing! Maybe what Jesus really meant was, "Do all that can be done first, before you come crying to Me."

In his book *The Meaning of Prayer*, Harry Emerson Fosdick asserted that there are some things God cannot do unless men will work.[1] It is more accurate to say that there are some things God *will not* normally do except through the ordinary means of human effort. He can multiply the loaves and fish but does not usually do so. Even when He did feed thousands, He still relied upon His disciples to distribute the miraculous food to the hungry crowd (Matt. 14:19; 15:36; Mark 6:41; 8:6; Luke 9:16). Food does not appear on the plate (or on the tongue) without some element of human effort, even when the food is miraculous. God can and occasionally does heal in an instant. Yet in most cases He chooses to work through the doctor. No human hand was needed to free Peter from his chains, but as long as Rhoda fails to unlock the door,

• • •

God's normal course is to provide through means, even when what He provides is in answer to prayer.

• • •

he cannot be restored to his friends (Acts 12:1–16). God's normal course is to provide through means, even when what He provides is in answer to prayer.

However, action can do little when prayer is what is needed. It is clear from Jesus' response that the problem of the disciples was one of faith, not effort. They had taken sensible action. These were not recreational boaters. They were fishermen who had experienced heavy weather before. The disciples had reached the end of their resources. They did the right thing when they brought the problem to Jesus.

Not Asleep at the Wheel

In order to understand Jesus' question, we must hear it in conjunction with the disciples' exclamation once the raging storm has been quieted: "Who is this? He commands even the winds and the water, and they obey him" (Luke 8:25). This reveals that the disciples' cry in the midst of the storm was an expression of need but not of faith. The fact that they seemed genuinely surprised at Jesus' ability to calm the storm suggests that their initial cry was more of an accusation than a plea for help. Indeed, the criticism that is merely implied in Luke's version is made explicit in Mark's account of this event: "Teacher, don't you care if we drown?" (Mark 4:38). The disciples accused Jesus of being asleep at the wheel. After all, it was because of Jesus that they found themselves in this predicament in the first place. He was the one who had urged them to cross over to the other side of the lake (Luke 8:22).

The disciples' complaint echoes one made by the children of Israel soon after Moses led them out of Egypt into the wilderness: "Was it because there were no graves in Egypt that you brought us to the desert to die?" (Exod. 14:11). Addressed to Moses, it was really a criticism of God's plan. In effect, they were saying, "Is this the best that you can do?"

We cannot help feeling at least a little sympathetic toward them. How often have we had similar doubts about the wisdom of God's plan for our lives? After careful prayer and thoughtful planning, we step out in a direction that seems to us to be the result of God's guidance. Yet instead of the success we had hoped for, we experience failure. Our circumstances do not improve; they grow worse. We do not understand how God can allow such things to happen. Could it be that we misread the signals? While that sometimes may be true of us, it was certainly not the case for the disciples. Jesus' plan was explicit: "Let's go over to the other side of the lake."

The explicitness of Jesus' statement explains His rebuke to them. He was not angry because they had disturbed His sleep. Neither was He impatient with them for seeking His help. He *was* disappointed with their lack of faith. Jesus was asleep in the boat, but He was not asleep at the wheel. Even if their little ship had gone down in the storm, the Master of the wind and waves would still have brought them safely to the appointed shore.

Yet those disciples enjoyed a clarity of purpose and an intimate experience of Christ's presence that we seem to lack. Our case is different than theirs. We too feel that turbulence of the storm, but we do not have the assurance of seeing Jesus' form sleeping peacefully in the stern of the boat. We have not heard Him name our destination. Instead, we do our best to determine His will and chart the course. We step out in faith.

Yet almost as soon as we have begun, the winds and waves of ordinary life beat us back and make the journey difficult. Unexpected problems arise and we are unable to make any headway.

. . .

Jesus does not always speak to the wind and the waves and quiet them. Sometimes the ship goes under.

. . .

As a result, we lose confidence both in ourselves and in God. We know what Jesus did for the disciples. Our uncertainty is whether He will do the same for us. Personal experience has shown that the story does not always end the same way. Jesus does not always speak to the wind and the waves and quiet them. Sometimes the ship goes under.

Drawing False Conclusions

It is essential that we understand this. Otherwise we may look to our circumstances as a gauge of God's attitude toward us. If we are healthy and things are going well, we will mistakenly think that this easy sailing is evidence of God's favor. Or the opposite may occur. When the skies darken and the seas begin to rise, we will question God's disposition toward us. This is especially true if we thought we were being guided by God. *If God really were guiding me,* we think, *things would be going more smoothly.* We will mistakenly interpret these troubles as a sign of divine displeasure. The truth is more subtle and in a way more unnerving. The storm does not mean that God has forsaken us, and smooth sailing is no guarantee that we are on the right course.

It is not always a blessing to get what you want. Sometimes it is a curse. After humanity set out to chart a course away from God, the worst consequence was to be "given over" to this sinful decision (Rom. 1:24). Theologian Helmut Thielicke explains that God "by no means judges merely—or better, he hardly ever judges, by smiting the transgressor with a stroke of lightning or some other disaster; on the contrary he judges him by letting him go in silence. Thus he allowed the people who built the tower of Babel to wreck themselves on their own godlessness. By doing what seemed to be nothing, he allowed the dispersion to fall upon them in their godlessness."[2]

In the same way, disappointment rarely means that God has turned His back on us. If the essence of disappointment lies in not getting what we desire, then we must conclude that disappointment is a familiar experience among God's people and the common lot of most of His best servants. Abraham died before receiving the promised inheritance in this life (Heb. 11:11–13). Jacob complained, "Everything is against me" when in reality it was "intended for good" (Gen. 42:36; 50:20). Moses pleaded in vain to be allowed to cross the Jordan with the Israelites. Their example is proof enough that hope deferred is not the same thing as hope denied.

Nor is God's refusal to fulfill our desire necessarily a sign of His rejection. In the garden of Gethsemane Jesus prayed three times that He be spared the cup of suffering. Although He was heard "because of His reverent submission," his request was denied (Heb. 5:7). The writer of Hebrews goes on to explain why: "Although he was a son, he learned obedience from what he suffered and, once made perfect, he became the source of eternal salvation for all who obey him and was designated by God to be high priest in the order of Melchizedek" (Heb. 5:8–10).

* * *

The Father's refusal to grant our requests is not an arbitrary decision.

* * *

It is significant that in His prayer Jesus spoke of a "will" of His own that differed from His Father's (Matt. 26:39; Mark 14:36; Luke 22:42). Jesus' desire to avoid the suffering that lay before

Him was so strong that He "offered up prayers and petitions with loud cries and tears." This preference for a "will" other than the one the Father had set before Him was not a sin. Neither was it wrong for Jesus to express His own preference in the strongest terms in prayer. The Father's refusal to grant our requests is not an arbitrary decision. It does not feel good, but it is always for our good. God does not dismiss our tears. He takes note of our desires (Ps. 56:8). When He thwarts our desire, it is for a good reason.

Knowing this may not make us feel better about the bitter taste of the cup that has been set before us, but it may help us to accept it. Like Jesus, we can learn to pray, "Yet not as I will, but as You will."

Fear, Envy, and Disappointment

An old cliché says, "I cried because I had no shoes, until I met a man with no feet." In reality, such comparisons rarely make us feel better. Instead of helping us appreciate our own circumstances, the fact that others face a worse plight is more likely to alarm us (see Job 6:22). We are at a loss to explain why such a thing should happen to them. We do not know what to say that will comfort them. Even worse, we find that the sight of their trouble makes us afraid for ourselves. If this can happen to them, what is to stop it from happening to us? The sight of a man without legs does not compel us to cherish the fact that we still have our feet, bare as they are. It makes us worry that we will lose our toes to frostbite.

Likewise, it is not always easy to "rejoice with those who rejoice" (Rom. 12:15). Instead we are more likely to look at the blessings of others and wonder why God does not do the same for us. Envy is at its most potent when it is aroused by those whose circumstances are similar to our own. Although I sometimes think I would like to be rich, I do not really envy Donald Trump and his millions. I do not see the things he has as being realistic aspirations in my life. No, it is my neighbor's slightly larger house or my colleague's promotion that sets me off. I am envious because someone else seems to be able to lose weight easier than me or because their son or daughter made the team and mine did not. Author Alain de Botton has noted, "We envy only those whom we feel ourselves to be like—we envy only members of our reference group. There are few successes more unendurable than those of our ostensible equals."[3] This envy is fueled by the perception that although we are equals, the course others travel appears to be easier than my own.

I could be right. Yes, I know God does not show favoritism (Rom. 2:11). But this does not mean that He treats everyone the same. What Paul says about spiritual gifts also applies to our natural circumstances: "he gives them to each one, just as he determines" (1 Cor. 12:11). We differ in height, weight, and appearance. We do not all have the same abilities, opportunities, or experiences. Some get cancer while others do not. Among those who get cancer, some survive but not all. Even those who share similar gifts and abilities do not necessarily enjoy the same degree of success. Doors may open for one that remain closed for another. Somebody just "happens" to be in the right place at the right time or finds himself in circumstances that lead to greater advancement, while another with similar or even greater ability is overlooked.

We have all experienced this kind of inequity in some form or another. Solomon complained, "I have seen something else under the sun: The race is not to the swift or the battle to the strong, nor does food come to the wise or wealth to the brilliant or favor to the learned; but time and chance happen to them all" (Eccl. 9:11).

Certainly these differences can be partially explained as the collateral damage of sin or as inequities suffered at the hands of a sinful society. They are a result of living in a fallen world. Karen Lee-Thorp observes, "Studies confirm what most of us intuitively sensed as children: Mothers and daycare workers smile, coo, kiss and hold pretty babies more than plain ones. Fathers are more involved with attractive babies."[4] In other words, from our earliest experience we soon discover that the playing field is not even. The attractive are better received. The wealthy have more opportunity to gain wealth. God is "fair" in His treatment, but biased sinful people are not.

Yet even here we cannot rule God out of the picture. Circumstances that seem arbitrary to us are a matter of divine design. We are right to assume that God has a hand in what happens to us, even when it is painful, difficult, or unfair. He is not the direct cause of all our suffering, but He is the gatekeeper through which everything must pass before it touches our lives. Our case is like that of the Old Testament patriarch Job. We are surrounded by a hedge of God's care and no one can lay a finger upon us without His permission (Job 1:10). Would Job have felt any better about his situation if he had known that God had set a limit on his trial and that Satan could only go as far as divine permission allowed? It may only have tempted him to echo the sentiment of Teresa of Ávila, who once complained to God, "If this is the way you treat your friends, no wonder you have so few." Yet God's sovereign purpose must be taken into account if we are to make sense of what happens to us.

On one occasion, when Jesus' disciples saw a man who had been blind since birth, they asked, "Rabbi, who sinned, this man or his parents, that he was born blind?" They reasoned that such things do not happen by chance. There must be cause and effect. Either the man or his parents must have done something to deserve such a fate. Jesus agreed with their basic assumption but not their conclusion. There was a reason. "Neither this man nor his parents sinned," said Jesus, "but this happened so that the work of God might be displayed in his life" (John 9:2–3).

The fact that God's strong hand is hidden from view does not mean it is absent. God is not asleep at the wheel. The captain of our souls has set the ultimate destination and charted our course. God's goal is to remake us in the image of His Son to bring glory to Himself. Everything we face in life is subordinated to this grand design (Rom. 8:29–30).

Does Jesus Care?

Yet the fact that Jesus had charted their course did not make the disciples feel any better about the storm. Mark's account of this incident captures the emotional inflection of their question and mirrors a fear we also feel: "Teacher, don't You care if we drown?" (Mark 4:38). It is not simply that God does not seem to help that bothers us; it is that He does not seem to care.

How are we to interpret Jesus' slumber during the storm? We should not see it as a sign of His absence or as a mark of His indifference. Rather, it was evidence of His peace. We usually think of the peace of God as something we experience. We see it as a peace that we receive—the peace that "transcends all understanding" (Phil. 4:7). It is that, but our experience of this peace must ultimately have its origin in God's own peace. This was the significance of Christ's slumber. Christ was not anxious or afraid. He was certain of the future. The wind and waves that were so troubling to His disciples could not reach Him. The nineteenth-century Scottish evangelist Henry Drummond observed, "Christ's life outwardly was one of the most troubled lives that was ever lived: tempest and tumult, tumult and tempest, the waves breaking over it all the time. But the inner life was a sea of glass. The great calm was always there."[5]

. . .

Although Jesus may seem to be removed from our circumstances, He is not unmoved by them.

. . .

The one notable exception to this was on the night before His death when Jesus prayed in the garden of Gethsemane. Scripture tells us that "he began to be deeply distressed and troubled" (Mark 14:33; Matt. 26:37). In that moment of dark distress, Jesus prayed while His disciples slept. He prayed not for His own peace but for ours. And the Bible tells us that He continues to do so today (Heb. 7:25). Although He may seem to be removed from our circumstances, He is not unmoved by them: "For we do not have a high priest who is unable to sympathize with our weaknesses, but we have one who has been tempted in every way, just as we are—yet was without sin. Let us then approach the throne of grace with confidence, so that we may receive mercy and find grace to help us in our time of need" (Heb. 4:15–16).

Here, ultimately, is the answer to Christ's question: "Where is your faith?" Our faith is not in the wind or the waves. It is not in the sails or the ship. Not even in the charts and maps or our skill as sailors. Our faith is in the God who became flesh and dwelt among us. Our faith is in the one who died on the cross and rose again. Our faith is in Christ.

6

Great Expectations or Delusions of Grandeur?

When Our Holy Ambition Goes Awry

"Whoever wants to become great among you must be your servant, and whoever wants to be first must be slave of all."

—*MARK 10:43-44*

"Mary, I know what I'm going to do tomorrow and the next day and the next year and the year after that. I'm going to leave this little town far behind and I'm going to see the world. Italy, Greece, the Parthenon . . . the Coliseum. Then I'm coming back here and I'll go to college and see what they know and then I'm going to build things. I'm going to build air fields. I'm going to build skyscrapers a hundred stories high. I'm going to build bridges a mile long."

So says George Bailey in director Frank Capra's beloved classic, *It's a Wonderful Life.* But George is wrong. He doesn't know what he's going to do tomorrow and the next day and the next year and the year after that. As it turns out, what he is supposed to do tomorrow is pretty much what he did today. God's plan for him is to do the ordinary thing, which of course is the last thing that George wants to do. Because George Bailey wants to lasso the moon.

Like George Bailey, we want to do something extraordinary. It is no wonder. This is what we have been told that we should do by our parents, pastors, and teachers. We have been urged to take our little lasso of Christian ambition in hand, shake it loose, and aim as high as we are able. We are told to expect great things from God and attempt great things for God. But for most of us the moon isn't what God has in mind. His plan does not call for us to streak into the heavens and leave behind a trail of glory. God's purpose is more down-to-earth. God's purpose for us is more mundane. At times we might even call it dull. And like George Bailey, we are not happy about it because we do not want to lead an ordinary life.

An Argument at Supper

We are not alone in having high aspirations. Jesus' disciples dreamt of doing great things for God too. Indeed, they were so intent on this goal that they lost sight of the thing that Jesus really wanted them to do. Nowhere was this more apparent than at the Last Supper. The Bible tells us that on the night that He was betrayed, Jesus celebrated a last Passover meal with His disciples. During the dinner "a dispute arose among them as to which of them was considered to be greatest" (Luke 22:24).

This was not a new dispute. The question of comparative greatness came up more than once among Jesus' disciples. Sometime after one of those arguments, which broke out while the disciples were on the road to Capernaum, James and John came to Jesus and asked Him to grant them the honor of sitting on His right and left hand "in [His] glory" (Mark 10:35–37). Their request outraged the rest of the disciples.

Now the quarrel had erupted again. The Gospel writers do not say what sparked it. Perhaps it was a result of the seating arrangements at the Passover meal. In the ancient world, one's place at the table was usually assigned by rank (Luke 14:7–11). We know that during the supper John reclined next to Jesus (John 13:23). Who sat on the other side? Peter or James must have seemed the most likely choices. Peter, James, and John were the "inner circle" among the Twelve. When Jesus was transfigured on the mountain, they were the only ones chosen to witness the event (Matt. 17:1; Mark 9:2). They were the only disciples permitted to see the healing of Jairus's daughter (Mark 5:37). They spoke to Jesus in private and asked Him to clarify His teaching (Mark 13:3–4). In a few hours these three would be the only disciples to witness Jesus' agony while praying in the garden of Gethsemane (Mark 14:33).

If anyone had a right to claim the other spot at Jesus' side during this meal, it would have been Peter or James. Yet Peter, whose name is almost always mentioned first among the disciples, was seated far enough away from Jesus that he had to signal John to ask the Savior a question (John 13:24). (Some scholars believe the table was "U" shaped, with Jesus on the left end seat and Peter across from Him in the seat of honor at the right end. If this scenario is correct, then the argument may have arisen because Peter claimed for himself the seat that others felt they deserved.) The location of James, whose name always precedes John's when the two are mentioned together in the Scriptures, is not even mentioned.

The other coveted honor at this meal was accorded to Judas, the one who would eventually betray Christ. Jesus handed Judas the piece of bread dipped in the dish, an act that identified him as an honored guest. Judas had to be within easy reach of Jesus in order for this to take place (John 13:26). This action must have surprised the rest of the disciples. Even though he was the group's treasurer and numbered among the Twelve, Judas was never one of the "inner three."

Perhaps John's presence at Jesus' side reminded the other disciples of his earlier request to be seated at Jesus' side in glory. Maybe it aroused fears that Jesus was going to grant John's request after all. James, the brother of John and one of the "Sons of Thunder," could have been angry because his brother had been granted a seat by Jesus' side and he had not. A few days earlier the crowd had welcomed Jesus into Jerusalem like a king. The disciples could sense Jesus' ministry rising to a climax. They assumed He was about to come into His own. Perhaps James took John's presence at Jesus' side as a signal that He was only going to grant half their request. Maybe Peter felt that Judas had been accorded an honor that should have been his. What is certain is the substance of the disagreement. They argued about which disciple should be considered the greatest.

> *What is certain is the substance of the disciples' disagreement. They argued about which disciple should be considered the greatest.*

Why Them and Not Us?

It is hard not to be embarrassed by such petty bickering. We wonder at its impropriety. *Don't they know what they must sound like to Jesus? Do they realize that they are witnessing the final hours before Jesus' suffering?* We roll our eyes and shake our heads. But that is only because we have come to this table as observers.

Let us find our own seat among them, however, and everything will change. Once we take our place in their midst we realize that this is no cautionary tale about the importance of politeness among believers or getting along. It is a mirror. This is an x-ray with the power to penetrate our Sunday manners and reveal the naked ambition that lurks in the interior of our souls. If we were to sit where these disciples sat, we would ask the question they ask: "Why him instead of me?"

In fact, this is a question that we do ask whenever someone else gets an honor that we feel we deserve. It is our complaint when another's achievement is recognized while ours goes overlooked. It is what we ponder when we interview for a job and fail to get the position or when the person we hoped to date goes out with someone else. *It could have been me*, we think to ourselves. But what we really mean is: "It *should* have been me."

Much of the time we are right to be disappointed. Disappointment may even be the necessary engine that eventually enables us to achieve our goal. Disappointment can motivate us to discover where we were lacking and try to close the gap. It compels us to ask again, to get the training we need, or maybe just to try a little harder. Disappointment in itself is not a bad thing. Neither is competition. There are many areas of life where competition provides us with a legitimate and powerful incentive to improve. Nobody questions the place of healthy competition on the playing field or in the marketplace. Some feel that it even has a place in the classroom.

Where They Went Wrong

But here at Christ's table it has no proper place, at least not in its present form. The competitive spirit among these disciples is fundamentally flawed. Their error lies not so much in the desire to be great or even to surpass one another, as in the means they employ to attain their goal and the standard of measure they use to evaluate their progress. Jesus diagnoses their problem in Luke 22:25 when

He says, "The kings of the Gentiles lord it over them; and those who exercise authority over them call themselves Benefactors."

Nearly every word of this statement is designed to deconstruct apostolic ambition and set it on a different path. Jesus compares the ambition of the disciples to the mentality of pagan kings. That Jesus would compare them to kings is not surprising. They are destined to sit upon thrones and reign as kings. He is about to confer a kingdom upon them (Luke 22:29–30). But the kingdom that Jesus has to offer operates by a radically different rule than any kingdom these disciples have experienced.

> • • •
> **Under Jesus' rule the way up is the way down. The greater my status is, the lower my seat.**
> • • •

In the kingdoms of the Gentiles, status is determined by power and position. The kings of the Gentiles "lord" it over their subjects. Under this kind of rule the only way to move forward is at the expense of others. When He notes that the kings of the Gentiles "call themselves benefactors," Jesus is not criticizing pagan rulers for wanting to do good to their subjects. "Benefactor" was a formal title. In this statement Jesus condemns the way of the world, a realm where titles mean everything and you know your worth by your place at the table. He gives notice that His kingdom will be governed by a radically different order. Under Jesus' rule the way up is the way down. The greater my status is, the lower my seat (Luke 22:26). The disciples missed this because they were operating under an inverted system of values, ignoring what was truly great and magnifying that which was of little consequence.

Spiritual Narcissism

The problem here is a kind of spiritual myopia. This is a condition that severely restricts our field of vision. It causes us to concentrate only on the present. Like the disciples, we want to know where we stand now in relation to others but can see only what is on the surface. Consequently, we make superficial judgments about the value of our own actions and those of others. What is more, our sympathies are skewed. We are interested primarily in ourselves. Spiritual myopia is symptomatic of an even worse condition—spiritual narcissism.

Narcissistic spiritual ambition is a point of view in which the highest goal is not to be good. Not even the best. Not really. What I really want is to be better than you. Narcissism has a toxic effect on spiritual ambition. It compels us to fulfill those ambitions at the expense of another. It poisons the delight we feel in accomplishing our goals. The pleasure we take in comparing ourselves to each other is not a joy in our own greatness so much as it is pleasure in being able to diminish someone else by the comparison.

Jesus is well aware of the true source of such ambition. He has experienced it firsthand. "Satan was the most celebrated of Alpine guides, when he took Jesus to the top of an exceeding high mountain and showed him all the kingdoms of the earth," G. K. Chesterton observes. "But the joy of Satan in standing on a peak is not a joy in largeness, but a joy in beholding smallness, in the fact that all men look like insects at his feet."[1]

The perspective Satan offers from this vantage point is a distorted one that is fundamentally at odds with Jesus. Christ alone knows the worth of the poor widow's small coin (Luke 21:1–4). He appreciates the real value of an act as simple as offering a cup of water to the thirsty (Matt. 10:42). What is significant to us is not necessarily significant to Him.

This dissimilarity of vision greatly increases our potential to misjudge the real value of what others do. It makes it highly likely that we will underestimate that which is most precious to God and overestimate what is unimportant. Our attempts to evaluate our own accomplishments are similarly flawed. We do not really know which acts of service have the greatest significance and which have the least. Such disparity of vision creates an insurmountable obstacle for spiritual ambition. It is hard to attempt great things for God when you cannot tell the least from the greatest.

Out of the Ordinary

Fortunately, Jesus' words and actions provide us with a set of corrective lenses and a remedy. "But you are not to be like that. Instead, the greatest among you should be like the youngest, and the one who rules like the one who serves," Jesus explains in Luke 22:26–27. "For who is greater, the one who is at the table or the one who serves? Is it not the one who is at the table? But I am among you as one who serves."

Jesus' reference to being like the youngest seems strange in an age that worships youth. As a general rule our culture thinks that it is better to be young than to be old. The young are the focus of attention in popular media and marketing, as well as in the church. But in Jesus' day the youngest was the least significant. Because David was the youngest of Jesse's sons, he wasn't even called in from the sheepfold when Samuel came to anoint Saul's successor (1 Sam. 16:11). Any who aspire to greatness under Christ's rule must be willing to aspire to the status of those who are usually regarded as least. It is not wrong to want to surpass all others if my aim is to excel in serving them.

John's Gospel completes the scene and reveals what Jesus meant when He said, "I am among you as one who serves." From John we learn that as the disciples argued, Jesus got up from the table, took off His outer garment, and wrapped a towel around His waist. He poured water into a basin and silently began to wash the disciples' feet, drying them with the towel that He had wrapped around Himself. When Jesus finished, He put on His clothes and returned to His place. "Do you understand what I have done for you?" He asked them. "You call me 'Teacher' and 'Lord,' and rightly so, for that is what I am. Now that I, your Lord and Teacher, have washed your feet, you also should wash one another's feet. I have set you an example that you should do as I have done for you" (John 13:12–15).

This, it turns out, is God's plan for us and like the disciples we are amazed by it (see John 13:6–8). We are dismayed, really, because this is not the great work that we had imagined for ourselves. We aspire to greatness and instead Jesus calls us to the everyday labor of a common household servant. We want to do something significant and He consigns us to ordinary work. This is the sort of menial work that the hotel housekeeper does when she pushes her lumbering cart piled high with towels, tiny bars of soap, and the strips of paper she puts over the toilet seat to prove that she just cleaned it. It is work that is quickly forgotten, even when it is done carefully. This is the kind of thing which, once it is finished, must be done again the very next day. We call it grunt work—drudgery. It is something one does for minimum wage or less. In fact, this is the kind of dead-end job that many of us go into the ministry to get away from. We leave it behind because we want our lives to "make a difference."

Writing about ethics, theologian Stanley Hauerwas notes that many find ordinary life "morally uninteresting."[2] They do not define the Christian life in relation to the humdrum but to revolution and conflict. Hauerwas argues that, instead, the emphasis should

> *We who are immersed in the everyday are often blind to its real spiritual value.*

be placed on the everyday: "For the moral significance of our lives is not constituted by moving from one significant social problem to another; rather, it depends on our willingness to work at being human through the manifold particularity of our lives. It is a matter of what we do with our time, whether we are willing to work to make our marriages worthwhile, how well we perform our everyday tasks."[3]

Hauerwas explains that this failure of vision is a result of our inability to "see" the world "under the mode of the divine."[4] As a result, we who are immersed in the everyday are often blind to its real spiritual value. Because it is common, it is not holy. Because it is ours, it is not significant. Instead of sanctifying the dull present, we dream of a more dynamic reality. Instead of living "through the manifold particularity of our lives," we ignore the ordinary in the hope that we will be called to some higher purpose. Because we are waiting for God to do some great thing through us, we are dismissive of the small thing that He actually intends us to do.

Extreme Unction

John speaks literally in John 13:12 when he says that Jesus "returned to his place" after washing the disciples' feet. But he also speaks symbolically. Jesus' actions were emblematic of what He had done and all He was about to do. After the dinner, there would be suffering and death. After death, there would be resurrection. After resurrection, a glorious ascension. Christ, who laid aside His glory, was about to take that glory up again. The one who was "in very nature God," yet "did not consider equality with God something to be grasped," was about to depart and reclaim the rights and prerogatives of His divine nature (Phil. 2:6). But before His departure, he gave His disciples this charge: "I have set you an example that you should do as I have done for you."

Down through the centuries, when the church has tried to follow this command literally, its tendency has been to rehabilitate it. The church resorts to gleaming linen and silver basins. It spruces up the chore of foot washing with a dash of poetry and a smidge of pageantry. The church's common practice has been to replace its slave's rags with a royal robe of dignity.

We are tempted to do the same when we try to obey Christ's command in principle. We put a shine on our service to Christ, gilding it with size, scope, or significance, thereby reassuring ourselves that there is some glory in what we are doing. Yet Jesus accepts our service. Not with grudging reluctance but eagerly. Not with bitter resentment but with a knowing smile. Jesus receives our meager service with deep affection, the way a mother might treasure a broken flower received at the hand of her child. He overlooks the tarnish of our cheaply bought basin. He ignores the threadbare linen and tattered corners of the towel. He reckons what has been done for others in His name as having been done to Him. Jesus opens wide His arms and gathers to Himself all our shabby acts of service.

The Parable of the Kite

When I was a boy I entered a kite flying contest sponsored by my Cub Scout troop. It was a mistake. I had no business being a scout in the first place. I was not interested in the values that lay at the heart of scouting. Mostly I liked the uniform and the way they saluted.

I had not paid attention when they showed us how to make a kite. I lacked the discipline required to carefully measure, cut, and assemble the materials. But I wanted to win so badly that I badgered my father with tears until he finally made the kite for me. I thought it was the prettiest kite I had ever seen. Crafted with an engineer's precision and decorated by the hand of an artist. I was certain that I would win.

The day of the contest my father came with me to the park to watch. The event began with a race to see who would be the fastest to get their kite into the air, followed by a contest to see whose would fly the highest. I dropped the ball of string when I released the kite, watching the cord string slip through my fingers as the diamond shape rose into a cobalt sky. The string unrolled so quickly that it burned my hand. The kite seemed to disappear from view. I could not make it out in the midst of all the other kites. Perhaps the plane I saw passing overhead had banked sharply to avoid it.

As the contest came to an end, I raced to bring the kite back to earth, wrapping the string around my hand and wrist. Mine was the last one to come down, further evidence to me that it had flown higher than all the rest.

Jesus has a keener eye than we do when it comes to our estimate of what we have done.

Once I had the kite in my hand, I looked anxiously at my father.

"Did I win?" I asked.

He shook his head no.

I was astonished. I clearly had the best kite. From my vantage point at the base of the hill, I was certain that mine had flown the highest. But my father had a keener eye. He knew better.

"Are you sure?" I asked.

He shook his head again.

"No, Johnny, you didn't win," he said, smiling affectionately.

I walked home with him dismayed, convinced that the contest had been rigged. It was only later, after I had grown in maturity, that I realized how mistaken my perception of the entire event had been. My kite had not flown as high as I thought. Even if it had, the glory would not have been mine but my father's. He made the kite.

Like my father, Jesus has a keener eye than we do when it comes to our estimate of what we have done. Like my kite, the glory for anything we might accomplish really belongs to Another. It is Christ who made us what we are. He has equipped us by His Spirit and empowered us to serve. Before we form too high (or low) an estimation of what we have done, we might do well to ask the same question Paul poses in 1 Corinthians 4:7: "For who makes you different from anyone else? What do you have that you did not receive? And if you did receive it, why do you boast as though you did not?"

With a basin and towel Jesus overturned the disciples' value system and called their judgment into question. He identified Himself with the role of a servant and with these strange implements topples all rulers, principalities, and powers (see Eph. 6:11–12). We too are confounded by this, disoriented by the growing conviction that things are not what they seem. Our heroes are not God's heroes. We are not the great ones we thought we were. Our successes are not as successful as we thought. But if that is so, then perhaps it also means that our failures are not so disastrous.

What is more, Christ promises that the day is coming when He will invest our service for God with His own glory and present it to the Father on our behalf. Only then, after what we have done has been bathed in the glow of Christ's love and grace, will we be competent to evaluate the true value of all we have done. Only there, shielded by the shadow of the cross, will we be confident enough to submit our service to the searching scrutiny of Christ. On that day we are liable to find that our measure of who is the greatest in the kingdom of God is wrong.

I suspect that we are in for a great surprise when we see the seating arrangement in heaven. I do not believe it will hurt us then to see where we really stand in relation to others. We will not be tempted to recite a list of our accomplishments or diminish those of another. Nor will we be surprised to learn where our place is located. Instead, we will acknowledge that God's judgment is right and laugh, perhaps a little sadly, at the foolishness of all our posturing on this side of glory.

7

Eat, Drink, and Be Hungry

When Our Appetites Are Too Big—or Too Small

**Blessed are those who hunger and thirst for
righteousness, for they will be filled.**

—*MATTHEW 5:6*

My mother was hungry most of her life. She cooked daily for us, but rarely sat down to eat. Unable to stomach the food she prepared for us, she ate her own meals at odd hours and nourished herself on a strange combination of the ordinary and exotic. One day she might eat a baked bean sandwich smothered in ketchup and the next broiled lobster.

Mother blamed her eating habits on a childhood of poverty. Born six years before the Great Depression, her first conscious memories were of hunger. Her family was so poor they often went days without eating. When there was food, there was little. Sometimes all they had to share between them was a can of beans.

Mother looked hungry, too. She was thin as a wraith much of her life, weighing an almost skeletal ninety pounds. Eventually, it seemed to me that this erratic diet consumed her, shredding her bowels and leaving her emaciated. Unable to keep down food on her own, she died in a hospital bed connected to tubes that provided nutrients for her weakened shell of a body.

My father, on the other hand, died from thirst. A large man with a hearty appetite, hunger was never his problem. In some ways, his experience was the polar opposite of my mother's. He was raised in comfort, though not in wealth. The son of a medical doctor, he observed the poverty of the Great Depression from a distance. To my knowledge, he never had to worry about his next meal.

I'm not sure when my father started drinking. In his teens, I suspect. By the time he reached adulthood, he was a full-fledged alcoholic. Eventually he couldn't start the day without a shot of the liquid napalm he purchased by the half gallon. Like my mother's strange hunger, his thirst for alcohol was the end of him. He spent the last days of his life waiting to have his dry lips moistened with a damp swab, unable to drink water because of his alcohol-ravaged kidneys.

The irony of their experience is not lost on me when I read the blessing Jesus pronounces on those who hunger in Matthew 5:6: "Blessed are those who hunger and thirst for righteousness, for they will be filled." Blessed are those who hunger? Blessed are those who thirst? Hunger and thirst signal the presence of need. They are symptoms of emptiness and unfulfilled desire. How can they be a source of blessing?

These words must have seemed equally strange to Jesus' listeners, who mostly lived in an arid world without indoor plumbing. For them the struggle to provide water was a daily occurrence. These were people whose next meal was far from certain. Hunger must have seemed a strange path to blessing to them.

Jesus and Hunger

In view of this it is important to recognize that Jesus was no stranger to hunger. He experienced it firsthand. The Scripture says that after fasting for forty days and forty nights, "he was hungry" (Matt. 4:2). But Jesus did not merely dabble in hunger, as if it were merely an item on the menu of human experiences that had been assigned to Him during the incarnation. He lived with its presence most of His earthly life. He grew up in a poor family (Luke 2:24; Lev. 12:8). During His earthly ministry, Jesus relied upon the generosity of others to provide for His material needs (Matt. 27:55). He felt compassion for those who came to hear Him preach and did not want to send them away without something to eat (Matt. 15:32).

What is more, much of Jesus' ministry took place in contexts where food was conspicuously present. He "came eating and drinking" and was a guest at dinners given in His honor (Luke 7:34; John 12:2). He so scandalized the religious leaders by sharing meals with sinners that they accused Him of being a glutton and a drunkard (Matt. 11:19). Food was also a feature of Christ's interaction with His disciples. The Lord's Supper, one of the two foundational traditions He passed on to the church, involved eating and drinking and was instituted at the final meal that He shared with His disciples before His arrest.

New Testament scholar Joachim Jeremias noted that this meal was "only one link in a long chain of meals which Jesus shared with His followers and which they continued after Easter."[1] According to Jeremias, food had eschatological significance in Jesus' ministry: "These gatherings at table, which provoked such scandal because Jesus excluded no one from them, even open sinners, and which thus expressed the heart of his message, were types of the feast to come in the time of salvation (Mark 2:18–20)."[2]

We can conclude from this that Jesus was no ascetic when it came to food. In Matthew 7:9–11 He used the analogy of ordinary hunger to illustrate the Father's compassion toward those who are His children: "Which of you, if his son asks for bread, will give him a stone? Or if he asks for a fish, will give him a snake? If you, then, though you are evil, know how to give good gifts to your children, how much more will your Father in heaven give good gifts to those who ask him!"

A Different Kind of Hunger

In view of this, how should we understand Jesus' statement that those who hunger and thirst are blessed? The fact that Jesus says that He is talking about a hunger and thirst for righteousness hardly clarifies matters. He seems to put the emphasis in the wrong place.

> • • •
>
> **We are tempted to think that righteousness is the condition we must be in to be blessed. Jesus says the opposite.**
>
> • • •

Why not say, "Blessed are the righteous" instead of "Blessed are those who hunger and thirst for righteousness"? Hunger and thirst imply a lack of righteousness. How can there be blessing in that? Jesus blesses what most of us would curse.

Clearly, our Lord is talking about a realm where the order of things is very different from the one with which we are familiar. Where righteousness is concerned, we would prefer to dwell on what we have rather than what we lack. Yet, according to Jesus, when we draw near to the kingdom, it is better to come empty than full. We are tempted to think that righteousness is the condition we must be in to be blessed. Jesus says the opposite. Righteous is the blessing. Jesus proposes an idea so radical, it turns our notion of God, righteousness, and blessing on its head. Hunger and thirst are the precondition.

Perhaps this is why eating and drinking played such a significant role in Old Testament worship. The shedding of blood was at the heart of Old Testament worship. The writer of Hebrews notes: "the law requires that nearly everything be cleansed with blood, and without the shedding of blood there is no forgiveness" (Heb. 9:22). But where there is shed blood there is also food. Priest and worshiper alike often celebrated God's provision of righteousness with a meal.

Old Testament worship also made special note of the prodigal nature of our appetite. The law of Moses, with its long list of clean and unclean foods, seems obsessively concerned about diet to the modern reader (Lev. 11). Some have interpreted these regu-

The desire to be filled was itself desirable. This was Jesus' point when He pronounced a blessing on those who hunger and thirst.

lations as primarily a regimen for healthy eating, as if this list were little more than a heavenly nutritional label. I think the message is much more serious. Such lists are a vivid reminder that we are addicted to a less wholesome diet. Righteousness is not our natural food. As a result, we are being consumed by our appetites. Like our first parents, whose hunger for forbidden food in the garden of Eden led to the ruin of our race, we too long for things which seem good, pleasing, and desirable but will eventually destroy us. What is worse, our efforts to sate our hunger and slake our thirst have ruined our taste for a better diet.

Our Spoiled Appetite

When I was young and wanted a cookie or a piece of candy before dinner, my mother would put me off with an argument that made little sense at the time. "You can't eat that," she would say. "You will spoil your appetite." Of course! Isn't that the whole point of eating? My mother's strange reasoning implied that an appetite was a good thing. It suggested that the desire to be filled was itself desirable. This too was Jesus' point when He pronounced a blessing on those who hunger and thirst. In this beatitude we hear an echo of the prophet's complaint, "Why spend money on what is not bread, and your labor on what does not satisfy? Listen, listen to me, and eat what is good, and your soul will delight in the richest of fare" (Isa. 55:2).

The Father and the Son agree in Their reproof to Eve and all her children: "Don't eat that. It will spoil your appetite." This is precisely our problem. While we need the drink that comes without cost and the bread that God alone offers, we do not always desire it. Our tastes have been captivated by other delicacies. Jesus pictured this in His parable of the great banquet (Matt. 22:1–14; Luke 14:15–34). The banquet is prepared and the guests are invited. Those who could be enjoying the feast lack only one thing. They are not hungry. Occupied with matters great and small, they are either too busy or disinterested to concern themselves with the table that has been laid for them.

This is often the case with God's people. Fortunately, God, in His mercy, takes steps to help us get over our taste for this food that cannot satisfy. The tool He uses, amazingly, is hunger. This was literally true for Israel during the years in the wilderness. In Israel's case, physical hunger was intended to make a spiritual point. This was a painful lesson, meant to be burned into their collective memory. "He humbled you," Moses explains in Deuteronomy 8:3, "causing you to hunger and then feeding you with manna, which neither you nor your fathers had known, to teach you that man does not live on bread alone but on every word that comes from the mouth of the Lord."

When the children of Israel lost their taste for God's daily fare in the wilderness, He let them learn from their hunger. They got the desire of their heart, only to discover that it turned their stomach. They ate the meat they craved until it came out their nostrils. In the end they loathed it (Num. 11:20).

The image is graphic and intentionally repulsive. It should resonate with us as we stumble through our own private wildernesses of sin. We log onto the Internet and feast our eyes upon things which sicken the soul. We turn on our televisions and get drunk on the wine of violence. We fill our stomachs with the bread of idleness and cast our leftovers to the poor, trying in vain to suppress the gnawing desires that eat at our hearts. No wonder Christ in His hunger quoted Deuteronomy 8:3 when Satan taunted Him in the wilderness (Matt. 4:4). Ours is a hunger no earthly bread can satisfy. We really don't want to spoil our appetite. And no wonder Christ sacramentalized our need for food and drink in the Lord's Supper, using hunger and thirst to point us to better fare (Matt. 26:26, 27).

God's Prescription for Our Hunger

Christ in His mercy deals with the prodigal nature of our hunger by submitting it to the strange order of the kingdom. The end result of this economy is foreshadowed in Mary's song in Luke 1:53, when she says that God has "filled the hungry with good things but has sent the rich away empty." This is not a mere redistribution of wealth in the socialist sense. Neither is it a reversal of fortune, even though what seems to be abundance turns to poverty and satiation leads to hunger. It is instead a return to reality as heaven defines it. The hunger described in this verse signals a restoration to the proper order. Those who have filled themselves with "what is not bread" go hungry. Those who have spent their labor on "what cannot satisfy" are sent away empty.

> ● ● ●
>
> **Hunger and longing serve as God's goad, prodding us toward a table spread with better fare.**
>
> ● ● ●

Mary's song looks ahead to a day of final judgment when the economy of the kingdom is established as the norm and all those who have refused God's gracious and persistent invitation to partake of better fare ultimately get their way. They are left with their preferred "treasure." They will be granted their heart's desire, an empty inheritance that turns out to be little more than a paradise of ashes.

But in this present age of invitation and grace, our hunger works for us. Hunger and longing serve as God's goad, prodding us toward a table spread with better fare. They are also a reminder that the "real" food we seek is bread from heaven. Jesus scandalized His contemporaries by equating their need for Him with their need to eat. A day earlier He had fed five thousand with five loaves and two small fish. The crowd pursued Him, but for the wrong reason, and Jesus accused them of seeing with their bellies rather than their eyes (John 6:26–27). Comparing Himself to the manna in the wilderness, Jesus declared, "Whoever eats my flesh and drinks my blood remains in me, and I in him" (John 6:56).

In our effort to distance ourselves from the Roman Catholic doctrine of transubstantiation, we Protestants have understood this claim primarily in negative terms. We spend so much energy emphasizing what Jesus does *not* mean that His words fail to whet our appetite. Our theological differences are not small. Still, the point Jesus makes in this assertion and later symbolizes in the Lord's Supper is even greater than the theological gulf between Roman Catholicism and Protestantism. Jesus' words remind us that Christ alone can sustain. All that we hunger for is to be found in Christ. The only way to be filled is to look to Christ.

However, it is necessary to add an important caveat here. We should not think that the Savior's promise of filling is a promise of fullness. Jesus does not promise satisfaction to us, as if it were some spiritual commodity to be offered to His customers. Hunger will continue to play a role in our experience. He does not want us to lose our appetite. In the strange economy of the kingdom, hunger and blessedness are bound together.

This is certainly true when it comes to our daily life. When Jesus teaches us to pray for our own needs in the Lord's Prayer, He instructs us to ask for "daily" bread (Matt. 6:11; Luke 11:3). Some scholars see this as an eschatological reference to the bread of the kingdom. Joachim Jeremias cites the fourth-century saint Jerome, who argued that the Greek word usually translated "daily" represented an Aramaic term that meant "for tomorrow." Jeremias explains, "Accordingly, Jerome is saying, the 'bread for tomorrow' was not meant as earthly bread but as the bread of life."[3] This bread is "the bread of the age of salvation" or heavenly manna.

Others understand the phrase in a more earthly sense. Daily bread is "our bread for subsistence" or "bread for the day that now exists."[4] Taken this way it is a request for the bread we need to survive. Yet either way one takes the phrase, whether literally or spiritually, it implies an ongoing experience of hunger.

Jesus Does Not Despise Our Hunger

Jesus extends the same compassion to us in our hunger and thirst that He exhibited to the multitudes. The One who was unwilling to send away hungry those who had come to hear Him in the wilderness knows that our hunger (in all its forms) is real and does not despise it. He healed lepers but also cared enough not to let the wine run out at a wedding (John 2:1–10). He raised the dead but also defended His disciples when they were criticized for satisfying their hunger on the Sabbath (Matt. 12:1–8).

It is true that Jesus chides us for our tendency to worry about what we will eat or drink and about what kind of clothes we will put on our bodies (Matt. 6:25–34). But this is not because He comes from heaven, a realm where food, drink, and clothing are of little concern. Jesus takes us to task precisely because He knows what it is like to make His dwelling here on earth. He shares our nature and is well aware that we are dependent upon food and clothing for survival. Far from despising these things, Jesus assures us that their importance is so self-evident it hardly needs to be said. The Father knows what we need before we ask Him (Matt. 6:8, 32). Theologian Helmut Thielicke observes, "Thank God that he accepts us just as we are, as living men, with great dreams, perhaps, and sometimes even with great ideas and achievements, but *also* with many *little* desires and fears, with hunger and weariness and the thousand and one pettinesses and pinpricks of life that fill even the lives of the great of this earth (one need only to read their memoirs)."[5]

At the same time, as important as these things are, Jesus is quick to remind us that there are other concerns that are even more important. When Jesus came to the well of Samaria, His hunger and thirst enabled Him to appreciate the thirst of the woman who came there to draw water (John 4:6–8). Yet He did not hesitate to point out to her that her natural thirst was merely symptomatic of an even deeper longing. "If you knew the gift of God and who it is that asks you for a drink," He told her, "you would have asked him and he would have given you living water" (John 4:10).

Bread and Forgiveness

Emptiness is a precondition to blessing. But Jesus' words to the woman of Samaria also make it clear that emptiness alone is not enough to guarantee that we will be filled. Those who hunger and thirst must also learn where to turn to satisfy their need. They must know that Jesus Christ is both the gift and the giver. Even more important, they must know the true nature of their need.

There is a hunger that bread cannot fill. There is a thirst that no earthly well can quench. Jesus implies as much in the Lord's Prayer when He links the petition for daily bread with a request for forgiveness. It is significant that Jesus taught His disciples to pray for bread *and* forgiveness (Matt. 6:11). In the Greek text, these requests are arranged in a chiastic structure that links them to each other. The relationship between these two requests is even clearer when we compare them with the fourth beatitude. It is those who hunger and thirst for righteousness that will be filled.

> • • •
>
> *The promise of righteousness is offered to those who are empty. It belongs to those who are aware of their lack.*
>
> • • •

We are sustained daily by a righteousness that comes to us as a gift from God through His Son. Just as our hunger is renewed each day, so is our need to forgive and to be forgiven. Just as we need bread to survive on a daily basis, we also need grace and forgiveness. In other words, our real hunger—our ultimate hunger—is for righteousness. "As universal as our need for bread is our need for pardon," Alexander MacLaren explains. "It is the first want of the spiritual nature, but it is a constantly recurring want, as this petition teaches us."[6]

This connection between forgiveness and hunger underscores an important dimension in the righteousness Jesus promises. It demonstrates that righteousness must be a gift before it can be a practice. The promise of righteousness is offered to those who are empty. It belongs to those who are aware of their lack. Like the bread promised by the prophet Isaiah, we cannot labor for this righteousness. Even if we wanted to work for it, we would not be able to expend enough effort to obtain it. If we wanted to buy it, we would not be able to offer enough money. We can't get it by loan. Even if we wanted to borrow this righteousness, we would not be able to find anyone willing to part with it. The only way to obtain righteousness is to receive it.

The language of filling also indicates that righteousness works from the inside out. This is particularly important, because we usually go about it the other way around. We try to work on it from the outside in. Righteousness for us is often a matter of externals. If we worship in the right building, perform the right rituals, wear the right clothes, and are seen with the right people, we are righteous. If we read our Bibles and pray in the morning, give a tithe of our earnings on Sunday, control our tempers and restrain our passions the rest of the week, we are righteous. In other words, we tend to approach righteousness as if it was some kind of mold. We try to pour ourselves into it, yet somehow we never seem to be able to fill up the edges. Or maybe it's a matter of control. We try our best to conform but somehow keep slopping over the sides.

If we listen to Jesus, we begin to understand why He attracted the sort of people who came to listen to His preaching: hookers and thieves, the outcasts and lowlifes. These were people who dwelt on the outskirts, in places where decent citizens refused to travel. If we dare to hear Jesus, we also understand why respectable, law-abiding people such as ourselves wanted to silence Him. It is because this word of Jesus has the power to strip us of all we thought we had achieved. This beatitude and these petitions rob us of what we thought we had acquired, leaving us naked, destitute, and empty. If we are to have righteousness as Jesus defines it, we must receive it like beggars and let it transform us from the inside.

Always Empty, Always Filled

But there is another, equally important truth implied in this language of hunger. Jesus' promises imply that true righteousness will leave us craving more. Here, more than anywhere else, the light of Jesus' truth reveals the cracks in our façade. We tend to think of righteousness as a standard. Like the little boy whose progress in growth has been marked inch by inch on the kitchen wall and compared to his father's height, we hope that we too will measure up someday.

In reality, there is no standard. Not in that sense. It is not as if there is only so much of God's righteousness, as if it were something we could accumulate and eventually exhaust. God has an infinite capacity for righteousness. Therefore, in a sense, so must we. Our destiny is not to "measure up" but to be filled. If God's capacity for righteousness is infinite, does it not seem likely that our capacity to experience and reflect that righteousness must also expand throughout eternity? If this is so, our experience of righteousness in eternity will be unlike the one we currently enjoy. On this side of eternity those who know Christ still retain the vestiges of their old nature. They sometimes sin and must be forgiven. They have an obligation to "put to death" whatever belongs to their sinful nature (Col. 3:5). They must "put off" the old self and "put on" the new self, "which is being renewed in knowledge in the image of its Creator" (Col. 3:10; Eph. 4:24). In eternity this will no longer be necessary. There we will not only enjoy a righteous standing before God, we will possess a righteous nature.

But there is no reason to think that this aspect of our nature will be static. Why should not the righteousness we have when we enter the eternal state continue to increase throughout eternity? If God's righteous character is infinite, there will always be a greater depth of God's righteousness for us to explore.

This must certainly be true of our experience of satisfaction in Christ. As our experience of Christ increases throughout eternity, so will our capacity to enjoy Him. Our destiny is not to be sated but to be filled. This is the secret to savoring the blessed hunger Jesus describes. Natural hunger is all about emptiness. The hunger Jesus blesses has more to do with our capacity to be filled. This is our lot. It is also our blessing. What is true of us this side of heaven is also true in a more perfect sense in eternity. We are always longing, always filled.

8

Take This Job

When Our Work Is Not Rewarding

**By the sweat of your brow you will eat your food
until you return to the ground.**

—*GENESIS 3:19*

A few years ago Mel Gibson made headlines when he co-
wrote and directed *The Passion of the Christ*, a graphic film
about the last twelve hours of Christ's earthly life. When
Pope John Paul II first saw the film, he reportedly declared, "It is as
it was." Billy Graham wept.

The film generated a firestorm of controversy when it was released, largely because of the violence it employed in its depiction of
the crucifixion. The film was so bloody that it was given an *R* rating.
But I think that one of the film's most remarkable scenes has nothing to do with violence. It is a scene where Jesus makes a table.

The scene is startling because of the contrast it creates. The
commonplace setting of Jesus at home living as son and carpenter is set against the somber background of His suffering as Messiah. This scene is all the more striking because it makes explicit a

fact to which Scripture merely alludes. Prior to the three years He spent in ministry, Jesus had an ordinary job like most of us.

When Jesus returned to Nazareth to preach, the people of His hometown referred to Him as "the carpenter" (Mark 6:3). This simple designation speaks volumes about Jesus' experience and indicates that part of what it meant for Jesus to grow "in wisdom and stature, and in favor with God and men" was the discipline of ordinary labor (Luke 2:52). Carpentry is not a skill that can be acquired in a few short days. Jesus learned the carpenter's trade from Joseph, His earthly father (Matt. 13:55). Years of practice would have been required in order to be considered a tradesman. Jesus spent most of His adult life working for a living.

The "Meaning" of Work

I came of age in a generation that believed that work should be "meaningful." I grew up thinking that my job should be significant and that I should enjoy my employment. My father did not entertain such fantasies. Like most of his generation, he thought of work as what you did to put bread on the table. It was nice to do something you liked, but not necessary. He would rather have been an artist but instead he spent the bulk of his career working as a graphic engineer for one of the major auto companies. His work was important to him. But I do not know that he enjoyed it.

I do know that my father was disappointed that he never achieved his dream of becoming a successful artist. His disappointment haunted me. I swore that I would not end up like him. So when I was in my late twenties, I quit my job at the auto company and pursued my dream of becoming a pastor, writer, and teacher. Unlike my father, I achieved my dream. Yet to my surprise and dismay, I found that having my dream come true did not make me immune to disappointment about my job. I love my work, but there are many days when I find it tedious. I believe that it is significant, but it is also filled with much that seems meaningless (or at least whose meaning is not readily apparent). Maybe you are disappointed with your job and find it offering little meaning and, at times, much routine. Meaning and disappointment are both intrinsic to the nature of work. We are created to live by our vocation, but must do so by the sweat of our brow. Work is our high calling, but it is also affected by the curse (Gen. 3:17–19).

Despite the effect of sin upon it, ordinary work continues to give meaning to our lives. Work originated with God. He is the first "worker" described in the Bible (Gen. 2:2). God's work extends beyond Creation. Jesus described His heavenly Father as one who "is always at his work" (John 5:17). Since we have been created in God's image, we should not be surprised to learn that we have been created to work. After God made Adam, He placed him in the garden of Eden "to work it and take care of it" (Gen. 2:15). Sin's entrance into the world has profoundly affected the way we experience work. But it does not diminish the dignity of work. Work predates the fall. Work as a vocation was part of God's design for humanity from the very beginning. The infinitive construction of Genesis 2:15 ("to work" and "to take care of") is the language of purpose. Our Creator is always at His work and we were likewise created to work. His work makes our role as workers meaningful.

Did Jesus Have a Low View of Work?

The fact that Jesus identified His work with that of the Father gives significance for the work we do. But it also begs a question. Isn't the work Jesus refers to in John 5:17 the work of ministry? It is true that Jesus is called "the carpenter" in Scripture, but only once.

There are no explicit examples of Him practicing this profession. Nowhere do the Gospels portray Him with tools in hand. Instead, we see Him acting as teacher and Messiah. The earlier period of His life is mostly shrouded in silence. The one brief glimpse we are given of His childhood emphasizes His ability to teach and His desire to be in His Father's house (Luke 2:46–50).

What is more, when Jesus called the disciples to follow Him, He seems to have called them *away* from ordinary employment. Peter and Andrew were on the job when Jesus came looking for them. While they were "casting a net into the lake," Jesus promised to make them fishers of men. Matthew 4:20 records their response: "At once they left their nets and followed him." Likewise, Jesus called James and John while fishing. Like their colleagues Peter and Andrew, "they left the boat and their father and followed him" (Matt. 4:22). It is easy to see why Levi would abandon the tax collector's booth when Jesus called him, since this profession was a byword for sin (Matt. 9:10–11; 11:19; 21:31–32). But there was no comparable stigma attached to fishing. The fact that the disciples left their boats and nets behind seems to imply that they were entering a calling that was "higher" than the one they had before. What is more, Jesus reaffirmed this call when Peter decided to take up fishing again after the crucifixion (John 21:1–18).

It must be admitted that Jesus' call did result in a change of vocational priority for these disciples. He invited them to leave their former work behind and follow Him into what might best be described as a kind of ministry apprenticeship. The demands of this new vocation would not allow them to continue in their old professions. This is often the case when it comes to ministry. Jesus called His disciples "laborers" and said that they were "worthy" of a wage (Matt. 10:10; Luke 10:7). The apostle Paul used this standard as the basis for his guideline to those who are responsible to provide financial support for the church's ministers (1 Tim. 5:17–18).

Yet Jesus' call to the disciples to leave their old work behind was not a reflection of vocational snobbery. His high regard for ordinary work is evident in His teaching. Jesus' parables are filled with examples from the

Jesus did not call His disciples away from their normal jobs to pursue a life of leisure or even one of holy seclusion but to engage in a different kind of work.

world of work, featuring farmers, household managers, builders, and slaves. Furthermore, Jesus did not call His disciples away from their normal jobs to pursue a life of leisure or even one of holy seclusion but to engage in a different kind of work. He used examples of ordinary work to help them understand the nature of the ministry to which they were now called. Peter, Andrew, James, and John were still going to be fishermen, but they now would engage in a different kind of fishing (Matt. 4:19; Mark 1:17). They were like laborers in the field (Matt. 9:37–38; Luke 10:2; John 4:35–38). They were responsible like "the faithful and wise servant, whom the master has put in charge of the servants in his household to give them their food at the proper time" (Matt. 24:45). In this new vocation, their work would be ministry and their ministry work.

The Spiritual Value of Work

There is a sense in which this is also true of all believers. It can be said of only a handful in the church that their regular work is the vocation of ministry. For most believers their ordinary vocation *is* their ministry. The spiritual value of work is central to the Bible's idea of vocation. It is obvious that work serves a practical purpose in our lives. By it we provide for ourselves and for our families. But commonplace work also has kingdom value. In 1 Thessalonians 4:11–12 Paul makes it clear that our work is an essential component of our overall testimony: "Make it your ambition to lead a quiet life, to mind your own business and to work with your hands, just as we told you, so that your daily life may win the respect of outsiders and so that you will not be dependent on anybody." Work is God's ordinary way of providing for our needs and enabling us to provide for the needs of others (Eph. 4:28).

It is tempting to compartmentalize life into zones that are either secular or sacred. The place of worship and spiritual activities like reading the Bible or prayer belong to the sacred. Work is relegated to the secular and marginalized. Such a view does not regard work as having any significant spiritual value. It is seen as a necessary evil, something that we must do to get by. Work is a dull necessity from which we must extricate ourselves as soon as possible. According to this view the ideal life is a life of leisure. Indeed, some of culture's least sophisticated (and least appealing) stereotypes of heaven revolve around exaggerated fantasies of leisure—floating aimlessly in the clouds strumming our harps. We may even consider our work to be an obstacle to spiritual growth. Perhaps if we spent less time at work, we would have more time to devote to God.

* * *

God's Spirit is as comfortable in the place of work as He is in the church.

* * *

The irony of such thinking, of course, is that we spend far more time at work than we do in church. In this compartmentalized view, most of life is lived in zones that are commonly regarded as secular. No wonder Eugene Peterson calls the world of work "the primary context for spirituality."[1]

The Bible makes it clear that God's Spirit is as comfortable in the place of work as He is in the church. What is more, work is a realm where God's Spirit is active.

Nowhere is this more evident than in the construction of the tabernacle. The book of Exodus describes how the Holy Spirit filled Bezalel "with skill, ability and knowledge in all kinds of crafts—to make artistic designs for work in gold, silver and bronze, to cut and set stones, to work in wood, and to engage in all kinds of craftsmanship" (31:3–5). The Spirit also equipped Bezalel's assistant Oholiab along with all the craftsmen of Israel, giving them the skills needed to make the tabernacle. This ability to work with wood, gems, and embroidery did not come in a flash but involved careful training (Exod. 35:34).

The only thing that separated this work from their ordinary employment was the end to which the result was devoted. Otherwise the effort and skill required by these builders, carpenters, and embroiderers was the same. The same Spirit who provided the skill for the construction of the tabernacle enabled these workers in their day-to-day employment. This is part of the Holy Spirit's work of bestowing what theologians have called "common" grace. It is the grace God gives for the common good and is distinguished from the special grace that leads to salvation. Common grace is a universal gift that reflects the goodness of God, who "causes his sun to rise on the evil and the good, and sends rain on the righteous and the unrighteous" (Matt. 5:45).

"Good" Work

This does not mean that all work is the same. Some work is better than others. I am not talking here about the kind of judgments most of us make about what makes one job better than another.

Our culture usually bases such distinctions primarily on the amount of income that can be earned or the prestige to be accrued from a particular profession. If the overall value of one's vocation is merely a function of fame or salary, it would seem that our culture believes that the stars of television and film, popular musicians, chief executive officers, and professional athletes make the greatest contribution to the collective good.

God, however, does not share our values. Neither does He necessarily value the work of a medical doctor or a college professor more highly than that of the factory worker on the assembly line or the person who works at the grill in a fast-food restaurant. Moreover, what constitutes "good" work is determined by a complex of factors that are more subtle than merely looking at one's potential for income or prestige. We have already seen two of the factors mentioned in Scripture. How does the work affect my family and others around me? One of the most fundamental reasons for working is to provide for our basic needs. Vocational employment is God's primary way of supplying daily bread and clothing (1 Tim. 6:8). By our work, we contribute to the common good.

But there is such a thing as "bad" work. The thief, drug dealer, and prostitute all engage in a kind of "work." The net result of their effort is profoundly destructive. It is also possible to do work that one would normally deem as "good" in a way that is unethical or soul-destroying. Good work can be done in a bad way. What is more, this responsibility to make sure that the work we do is "good" work is shared. The relationship between employer and employee is one of mutual obligation. This mutual responsibility is reflected in the biblical principle of compensation succinctly captured in Scripture by the repeated statement: "The worker deserves his wages" (Luke 10:7; 1 Tim. 5:18). Although the notion of an earned wage is incompatible with the Bible's doctrine of salvation, it is foundational to its theology of work.

Both Testaments teach that one who labors is owed an equitable wage. The law of Moses warned that the failure to pay the "hired man" his wages in a timely manner was a sin (Deut. 24:14–15; the Hebrew term used in this verse refers to one who renders services in return for pay). This law was later reaffirmed by James in the New Testament (James 5:4). The payment rendered to the worker is not charity. Jesus makes it clear that the laborer *deserves* the wage that is owed. However, there is a reciprocal obligation reflected in these verses. The one who has hired the laborer has a responsibility to recompense the workman for what has been done. But the laborer also has a duty. The worker is worthy of the wage because it is commensurate with the effort that the employer expects to be exerted (Col. 4:1).[2]

Parables of the Workplace

Two of Jesus' parables shed interesting light on the question of what is owed in the workplace. The parable of the workers in the vineyard and the parable of the talents both have employment and evaluation as a backdrop. I am not suggesting that these parables were primarily meant to serve as a guide to employers. They are intended to shed light on God's grace and the nature of the kingdom of God. Yet Jesus' use of the employer/employee metaphor as a backdrop does shed some light on His assumptions about this realm of life.

In the parable of the workers in the vineyard, God is portrayed as one who generously rewards those who labor (Matthew 20:1–16). This parable describes a shocking grace by which those who have invested less labor (because they came to the field later) receive the same reward as those who have had to endure the heat of the entire day. To suggest that employers ought to pay every employee the same wage would go far beyond the scope of this parable. Yet it would not be too much to say that a grace-informed ethic in the workplace would be one which has generosity and kindness as its dominant features.

Jesus seems to acknowledge that the owner enjoys a certain measure of sovereignty when determining what to pay. The vineyard owner asks: "Don't I have the right to do what I want with my own money?" (Matt. 20:15). The implied answer is "yes." In other words, an employer has the authority to determine the level of expectation for those who work as well as the reward as long as both fall within the bounds of equity. It was entirely proper for the vineyard owner to expect some workers to labor for an entire day and others to labor for only an hour and then pay both the same. This was the employer's "right." However, it is important to note that, in the context of the parable, the only right asserted here was the right to be more generous than expected. The parable assumes that those who worked the entire day were paid what they deserved. Old Testament law made it clear that the vineyard owner did not have the right to expect the workers to labor an entire day and only pay them an hour's wage.

The theme of expectation is further emphasized in Jesus' parable of the talents (Matthew 25:14–30; Luke 19:12–27). Here Jesus tells the story of a man who entrusts his property to four stewards before setting out on a journey. Upon returning from his trip, the man calls his servants to "settle accounts" with them. In Luke's version, the man is described as a "king" and those who are entrusted with talents as "servants." This is another reminder that these parables were not meant to provide detailed guidance about employer/employee relationships. The parable of the talents, like the parable of the laborers, is a parable of the "kingdom."[3]

Yet it is just here that the parable provides an important insight. Ac-

• • •

According to Jesus, evaluation and reward are consistent with kingdom values.

• • •

cording to Jesus, evaluation and reward are consistent with kingdom values. When Christ returns He will assess the performance of those who have served Him. What is more, this parable suggests that His evaluation will be based on a standard of expectation. The master tells the "wicked, lazy servant" what he *should* have done. (One cannot help noting that the lazy servant's assessment of his own performance differed significantly from that of his master!) This is the language of duty and accountability. It assumes that the servant owed his master a certain level of performance in the execution of his duties.

Rendering What Is Due

It is reasonable for an employer to expect employees to perform their duties satisfactorily. It is appropriate for them to set the standard by which satisfaction is measured. Even more, it is entirely reasonable for an employer to expect those who work for them to cheerfully seek to meet the standard. God's expectation of Christian slaves under the authority of a master is also His expectation of believers who voluntarily place themselves under the authority of an employer: "Obey them not only to win their favor when their eye is on you, but like slaves of Christ, doing the will of God from your heart. Serve wholeheartedly, as if you were serving the Lord, not men, because you know that the Lord will reward everyone for whatever good he does, whether he is slave or free" (Eph. 6:6–8).[4]

The employee, like the slave, is under authority. It is true that the employee differs from the slave in a fundamental and important respect —he or she can choose to break the relationship at any time and seek employment elsewhere. Yet it is the voluntary nature of this relationship that is the very thing that makes the employee responsible to the employer. As theologian John Murray explains: "A freeman is not, of course, bound to the service of one man as the bondservant may be. But when he undertakes to serve a master the obligation of service ensues."[5]

Murray goes on to point out that "obedience" for the Christian involves more than mere compliance with the wishes of the one who is in authority. The biblical concept of obedience encompasses attitude as well as action. He notes that this expanded definition of obedience is liable to be distasteful to the modern mind, which values its freedom. Yet, according to Murray, it is not freedom but integrity that is at the heart of the matter and attitude is an essential element in integrity.[6]

In Christ all are under authority because all are servants of one Master. Those who expect the obedience of another are accountable to the Lord for the manner in which they discharge their oversight. Those who are under authority are to render "what is due" as if it were owed to Christ. For the Christian employer and the Christian employee alike the same rule applies: "Whatever you do, work at it with all your heart, as working for the Lord, not for men, since you know that you will receive an inheritance from the Lord as a reward. It is the Lord Christ you are serving" (Col. 3:23–24).

When it comes to what the employer owes, there is more due to the worker than a wage. Businessman and author Max DePree has written eloquently about what leaders owe the organizations they serve. One dimension of this debt has to do with its culture, an element of which is what we normally call the "working environment." DePree explains that leaders are responsible to promote civility and values: "In a civilized institution or corporation, we see good manners, respect for persons, an understanding of 'good goods,' and an appreciation of the way in which we serve one another."[7]

The Old Testament example of Boaz and his treatment of Ruth provide a good model of this. Ruth was one of the poor who benefited from the social safety net provided by the Mosaic Law. The law commanded God's people not to harvest the corners of their fields or to pick up the grain that dropped to the ground during the harvest but to leave them for the poor and the alien (Lev. 19:9–10). They followed behind the harvesters to pick up the grain that dropped to the ground. Boaz gave Ruth permission to share the servants' food and drink, an indication not only of his concern for her but also of his general commitment to provide humane working conditions for his own workers (Ruth 2:9; 14). This went beyond providing food, drink, and a place to rest. Boaz also charged his servants not to molest or verbally mistreat her (2:15–16). This reflected an overall determination that the working conditions be free from sexual and verbal harassment.

Work and the Rhythm of Life

Work is an important facet of life, but it is not life's only dimension. In the beginning God set the pattern for work, but also for rest. Genesis 2:2 says that on the seventh day God rested from all His work. Obviously God did not rest out of need. He did this to establish one of the basic rhythms of Creation. God later institutionalized this rhythm in the Mosaic Law, which required His people to observe the Sabbath. One of the reasons God made this a point of law was to ensure that man and animal were both granted relief from the burden of their work (Ex. 23:12).

The necessity for such a law serves as a grave reminder of the potential for God's gift of work to be distorted. It is sobering to consider that the same God-given ability to embroider that the Holy Spirit sanctified in the building of the tabernacle is abused by those who enslave workers in sweatshops that make much of the clothing that is worn today. Work can give purpose to life and serve as God's way of providing for our needs, but it can also become an idol. We may love our work more than our families. We may love our work more than we love God, who gave us the ability to work. Work is important, but there are some things that are more important than our work.

Pausing from work serves a dual purpose in the spiritual realm: It is an expression of our dependence on God and a reminder that our greatest hope lies in the future.

The discipline of pausing from work serves a dual purpose in the spiritual realm. It is an expression of our faith in God and dependence upon Him. In the wilderness God miraculously preserved the manna that was collected the day before the Sabbath so that Israel would have enough to eat. This is one of the fundamental lessons of the Sabbath: God will take care of us. Just as we do not live by bread alone, we do not live by the strength of our own hand. Work is God's ordinary means of providing for our needs, but it is important to recognize the distinction between *means* and *source*.

The Sabbath principle also serves as a reminder that our greatest hope lies in the future. As the writer of Hebrews puts it: "There remains, then, a Sabbath-rest for the people of God; for anyone who enters God's rest also rests from his own work, just as God did from his" (Heb. 4:9–10). The regular cycle of work and rest, which sometimes feels monotonous, points our expectation toward the future. No matter how much we enjoy our work, it will not ultimately satisfy us. We should not trust in our work nor should be put our hope in the things we obtain as a result of our work. If we are weary of our work, the rest of Sabbath is a reminder that the burdens we now experience will one day be lifted. There is a better rest yet to come. There is also better employment. The rest for which we wait is not the cessation of activity.

Like the cycle of work and rest reflected in the Sabbath, there is a cycle to our vocational life. This normal trajectory reflects an important and sometimes painful truth. As we age, our capacity to perform changes and often diminishes. Even if we become masters in our craft, eventually a day comes when we can no longer do the things we once did. This normal progression is reflected in the Mosaic Law which required the Levites to retire at the age of fifty. One obvious reason for this was the demanding nature of their work. Much of what the Levites did would be considered manual labor. They put up and took down the tabernacle along with all its furniture (Num. 1:50–53). They handled the oxen and the wagons used in its transportation (Num. 7:6). This was work best suited for the young. Retired Levites continued to serve as a valuable resource, mentoring and assisting their younger counterparts. But they were no longer permitted to do their regular work (Num. 8:24–25). In work as in everything else, one generation eventually gives way to another.

God's Plan and Ours

The idea of vocation is grounded in the assumption that God is sovereign over our career. Those who approach their work as a divine vocation know by experience that even when we make plans, it is God alone who determines our steps (Prov. 16:9). His plans are not always our plans. Only a sense of God's purpose in our work can turn a job into a vocation.

My friends Ron and Margaret are the best example I know of this. My wife and I first met them more than thirty years ago. They managed the apartment complex in which we lived. Ron and Margaret are polar opposites in many ways. Ron is big and Margaret little. Margaret is an avid reader, Ron not so much. But they both have a ringing laugh and a fierce devotion to Jesus Christ.

Ron's ambition was to be a successful entrepreneur. A gifted salesman, he dreamed of starting his own company. Margaret dreamed of owning a home. It didn't even have to be a big one. A small house would do just fine. Most people dream of being rich, of course, but Ron's desire to succeed was driven by stewardship, not by luxury. He wanted to be the kind of person through whom God channels blessings. In my view, Ron is the sort person who *should* be rich. But he wasn't the sort of person who gets rich, at least not in Detroit's struggling economy in the 1980s and '90s.

Ron did start a business. And Margaret got her house. But the failing Detroit economy eventually dealt a death blow to their dreams. Ron's business is gone now, a casualty of the bad economy. Margaret's house is gone, too.

When Jane and I visited them recently, our friends had come full circle. They now live in and manage an apartment complex, working for the kind of man that Ron once felt he was called to be. They showed me their employer's office while I was there. He is a real Christian who sees his wealth as a stewardship. A verse of Scripture is written in gold letters on the wall behind his chair. It reads, "What shall it profit a man, if he shall gain the whole world, and lose his own soul?" Ron empties his trash.

Ron and Margaret's story is like that of many I know. They chart a course for themselves only to reach an unexpected destination. They do not get the job they want. Their dream does not come true. Those who say that you can be whatever you want as long as you believe in yourself are wrong. Things do not always go according to plan. I am tempted to say that they *never* go according to plan, at least not according to our plan.

But if you thought this was a story about failure, you would be wrong. It is true that Ron and Margaret did not end up in the place they hoped to be. But they did end up where they belonged. By God's grace, they reached the place of God's appointment. Managing the apartment is not merely a job; it is their gift. The job itself is God's gift to my friends, His way of providing for their needs in a difficult economy. As Ron and Margaret do their work, they become God's gift to the residents, from the care Margaret uses when she selects candy for the dish in lobby, to the trash cans Ron empties each night. The completion of each menial task is their way of uttering a blessing. It is their spiritual vocation.

In the end the difference between a career and a vocation is really a matter of perspective. In a career, we look to find the kind of work for which we are best suited and which best suits us. In a vocation, we look to find God in our work.

9

The Trajectory of Worship

When We Hate the Music at Our Church

**Offer your bodies as living sacrifices, holy and pleasing
to God—this is your spiritual act of worship.**

—*ROMANS 12:1*

The first time I can remember singing from a hymnal was in 1972. It was the year between high-school graduation and college, the year I got my first full-time job. That year, my mother's health began to fail and my world shifted on its axis as I started to follow Jesus. That was the year I began to attend Glad Tidings, a plain-looking concrete bunker of a church, whose colored windows reminded me more of ashtray glass than cathedrals.

Glad Tidings was a Pentecostal church, but of the reserved variety. Their Azusa Street brethren, ravished by the Spirit, might whoop and dance and swoon in ecstasy, or speak in the mysterious language of men and angels. But not the folks at Glad Tidings. It's not that they didn't believe in such things. They were convinced that God had the power to interrupt the service at any moment. He might send them all into a fit of shouting that could last for days. Indeed, they prayed for such things to occur. But they never acted as if they actually *expected* they would.

Most of the time, or so it seemed, God respected their suburban sensibilities and kept a polite distance. But every so often, the Spirit would stir the congregation the way the angel stirred the waters of Bethesda, and one or two voices would cry "Glory" or "Amen." They were always the same voices, of course. They never made this declaration in any sort of volume that would disturb our suburban decorum. But it was loud enough for all of us to hear. Just loud enough to let the rest of us know that there was glory afoot.

Worship in Two Voices

They were less self-conscious about singing. Three or four times during the service the entire congregation reached for the old red hymnals in the pew racks and gave voice to their faith. Its dog-eared pages were illuminated by the penciled scrawls and stick figures of bored children. The stanzas below those hieroglyphics depicted the pilgrim life of Jesus' followers as one of wandering and weariness, tears and tarrying.

We were passing through the valley.

We were camped on the banks of the river.

We were sinking deep in sin.

The hymn writers helped us to get our bearings by pointing to the milestones along the way.

We were at Bethel with Jacob.

We were drinking water from the rock with Moses.

We were in the garden with Jesus.

I would not describe the melodies of those old hymns as pretty. They often seemed strange to me, as archaic as the shape note harmonies of *The Sacred Harp* from which many of them were originally hewn. They exuded a kind of musty charm for me, the way my grandmother's house did with its ancient wood and iron stove. Something about them reminded me of the songs my father and my uncles sang after they had drunk too much beer. Songs with titles like "Let Me Call You Sweetheart" and "On the Road to Mandalay." Those old hymns rolled along with a rhythm that was so predictable, you didn't need to know the words or the melody to sing them. If you knew one hymn, it seemed, you knew them all. And if you didn't know it, you only had to wait a stanza or two to sing it like you knew it.

The songs we had sung the night before at the Lost Coin Coffee House were different from the hymns we sang in church. The Lost Coin was located in the Sunday school building just across the parking lot from the church. At the Lost Coin, we worshiped God with campfire rounds, led by a gangly guitar player named Mike who prayed daily for the salvation of Bob Dylan and George Harrison. The songs we sang at the Lost Coin were simpler, based on a handful of chords and a seemingly endless repetition of the chorus. But we didn't mind. If anything, their simplicity made them even easier to sing than the old gospel songs. We sang them with great enthusiasm. We clapped. We stomped. We sang in antiphonal rounds. We mirrored the meaning of the words with hand gestures. If someone had taken the words of Psalm 119 and fit them to the tune of "Bingo" ("There was a farmer had a dog and Bingo was his name-o"), we would have sung it. All 176 verses of it.

A Different Kind of Music

The songs we sang at the Lost Coin were fun. But fun is not the word I would use to describe those old hymns of the church. If the campfire rounds we enjoyed at the coffeehouse taught us that we could lift our voices in worship, those old hymns taught us how to lift our gaze. The God spoken of in those songs was not fun but immortal and invisible. He was so holy we had to say it three times. "Man of Sorrows, what a name," we cried, "Hallelujah! What a Savior!" Those were the kind of songs that caught in your throat and moved you to tears. The kind that made you stand a little straighter and sing a little louder.

> *I have reached that stage in life where most of the music I hear in church annoys me. Anecdotal evidence suggests that I am not alone in my disappointment.*

Now, thirty-eight years later, I find that I have reached a stage in life where most of the music I hear in church is "their" music, whoever "they" are. That is to say, I have reached that stage in life where most of the music I hear in church annoys me. I do not mean to be a music snob. Indeed, I think of myself as an eclectic. I was raised on Bix and Beethoven. I came of age in the era of the Beatles. The stations on my car radio are set to classical, country, oldies, rock-'n'-roll, and even Christian music. I think of myself as someone who has been baptized by immersion in the waters of musical diversity. Yet somehow when Sunday comes, all my musical sophistication dissolves and I am reduced to that most primitive test of aesthetic values: "I may not know what art is, but I know what I like." Or rather, "I may not know what worship is, but I know what it isn't." When the worship leader reminds me that worship "isn't about me," I try to take it to heart. I really do. Nevertheless, more often than not, I walk into church hoping to be a worshiper but leave a curmudgeon. A chastened curmudgeon. A repentant curmudgeon. But a curmudgeon nonetheless.

Anecdotal evidence suggests that I am not alone in my disappointment. Most of the people I know are disappointed with their worship experience. If the church service is not too contemporary, then it is too traditional. The sermons are too long, or else they are too short. If it is not too upbeat, then it is too slow and stodgy. While the reasons for our dissatisfaction are not hard to identify, they are extremely difficult to resolve because the solution that satisfies one worshiper often alienates another.

Worship's True Trajectory

I have concluded that the root of our problem is more a matter of vertigo than aesthetics. What we need is not a change of tune, so much as it is a reorientation to worship's true trajectory. We tend to view worship as something that moves from earth to heaven. We think of worship as something which originates with us. It is our gift to God. Perhaps this is why so many of us are conflicted about it. We consider worship to be an expression of our own personal devotion. So when the musical style or some form of expression gets in the way, we don't really feel like it is *our* worship at all. It is someone else's idea of worship—the worship leader's, perhaps, or that of the majority—but not our own.

The biblical portrait of worship moves in the opposite direction. The trajectory of heavenly worship begins with God and descends to the earth. This trajectory is reflected in Psalm 150, where praise begins in the heavenly sanctuary and resounds throughout the domain of God. From there it is taken up by those on Earth, who praise God with a variety of instruments and with dancing, until "everything that has breath" praises the Lord (Ps. 150:6).

This is the same trajectory of worship that we find described in Revelation 5:12–13. John, who has been caught up to heaven to see an innumerable multitude of angels and saints surrounding the throne of God, hears the angels declaring the worthiness of the Lamb "to receive power and wealth and wisdom and strength and honor and glory and praise!" Revelation 5:13 continues: "Then I heard every creature in heaven and on earth and under the earth and on the sea, and all that is in them, singing: "To him who sits on the throne and to the Lamb be praise and honor and glory and power, for ever and ever!"

Worship as Answering Speech

In his book *Working the Angles,* Eugene Peterson makes an observation about prayer that applies to worship in general. "Prayer is answering speech," Peterson writes. "The first word is God's word. Prayer is a human word and is never the initiating and shaping word simply because we are never first, never primary."[1] Worship is by nature answering speech. Like a musical instrument in which all the other strings resonate when one string has been plucked, earthly worship resonates with the worship of heaven.

Worship is not our attempt to project our voices so that they will be heard in heaven. Neither is it a performance executed on the earthly stage for the benefit of a spectator God. It is certainly not something we do primarily for ourselves—as if it were a kind of spiritual self-amusement or spiritual entertainment. In a sermon entitled "Praise, One of the Chief Employments of Heaven," eighteenth-century theologian Jonathan Edwards explains, "Let it be considered that the church on earth is the same society with those saints who are praising God in heaven. There is not one church of Christ in heaven and another here upon earth." This means that when the church gathers for worship, it engages in a heavenly activity.

The worshiping church does not merely imitate what goes on

in heaven. It participates with heavenly worship. Like one who walks into the church sanctuary after the service has started, those who worship on earth move into something that is already in progress in heaven. We take up a theme that was begun by others before the throne of God and add our voices to theirs. Consequently the worshiping church is part of a much larger congregation. It is one that includes patriarchs and prophets, saints and angels. No wonder Jonathan Edwards called worship "the work of heaven" and observed, "[I]f we begin now to exercise ourselves in the work of heaven, it will be the way to have foretastes of heaven."[2]

Worship, Music & Mood

Another reason we react so strongly to worship is a result of our tendency to identify worship almost exclusively with music. The biblical view is much more expansive. Worship has to do with all that we owe and offer to God. All our thoughts, words, and actions are part of the offering of our whole self (Rom. 12:1–2). In this view, we are never out of the place of worship. No ground is common. Every place is a sanctuary and every thought, word, or deed an act of devotion.

Yet for most Christians worship primarily is what we do when the church gathers together and specifically when the church lifts its voice in song. When this happens, we do not always like what we hear. The reasons for our reaction are complex. In his book *Resounding Truth*, Jeremy Begbie writes that music not only reflects a social and cultural order, it is also embedded in what he calls a "sonic order." Music, he says, "involves the integrity of the materials that produce sound and of sound waves, the integrities of the human body, and the integrity of time."[3]

What is more, our response to music is a reflection of our life experience and our culture. Begbie explains, "When we hear music a whole range of elements are pulled together—in particular, our state of mind and body, memories and associations, social and cultural conventions, and other perceptions that come along with the musical sounds. Together, these greatly affect the meaning the music will have for us."[4] Music especially has an effect on our mood. Begbie calls music "one of the most emotionally potent media we know."[5] He also notes that music's primary function in today's culture is mood management. Its primary purpose is to create ambience for some other activity.[6]

This is also true of the church; only in our case this "ambience" is called worship. As a result, what we call "worship" today is often identified as a particular kind of mood. Contemporary worship suffers from a kind of emotional bias. This was driven home to me recently during the convocation service at the Christian college where I teach. Every fall the faculty and administration put on their academic gowns and march into the auditorium. We sit on the platform in full view of the student body and try to look scholarly as Scriptures are read, hymns sung, and the president greets the students.

We usually sing the same hymns every year, including the old school song (a beloved remnant of the nineteenth century that sounds like a football cheer), the new school song (which is hated by most because of its pompous tone and unsingable meter), and listen to the same Scriptures. There is a kind of warm comfort to the whole service. If it is not very interesting, it is at least familiar. That is to say, the service has the same soporific effect as the typical church service, which also means that the alert student who scans the rows of faculty seated on the platform may notice the occasional head bob or eyelids close.

This year, for me at least, the service's usual tranquilizing effect was accompanied by a general sense of melancholy. I am not sure what brought it on. As I sat on the platform, I found myself brooding over the number of times I had sung the same hymns and listened to the same remarks. I looked at the cheering students and wondered how soon it would be before their freshman zeal faded. I thought about colleagues who had sat with me on the platform in years past and were now gone. Some had moved on to other places of work or ministry, some retired, and a handful have gone home to be with the Lord. Apparently all of this was reflected in my facial expression, because as I made my exit during the final processional, a student shouted, "Smile Dr. Koessler! Jesus loves you."

I have no doubt that the student who urged me to change my disposition was motivated by an interest in my well-being. But for me this incident underscored a common problem in worship. It reflects the kind of emotional tyranny one often experiences in church. I am not necessarily talking about the tempo of the music, although this bias is sometimes reflected in the tempo. I am talking about its emotional tone. The culture of evangelical worship is disproportionately upbeat and shows little tolerance for grief or ordinary sadness. It has even less patience with boredom. Come to the place of worship on any Sunday and you are liable to be subjected to a tongue lashing by some well-meaning worship leader who urges you to leave your troubles at the door, plant a smile on your face, and put some enthusiasm into your singing.

• • •

The pressure for Christians to present a bright and cheery face to the world does not come from God. If you doubt this, read the Beatitudes.

• • •

What drives this? As someone who has spent years standing

before the congregation, I can tell you that it is more fun when the congregation is happy. Image may also have something to do with it. The church today is a marketed commodity and a gloomy church is a hard sell. What I am certain of is that this pressure to present a bright and cheery face to the world does not come from God. If you doubt this, read the Beatitudes. They tell us what kind of people Jesus welcomes into His presence. It is a short list of the world's most miserable—the despised, the forlorn, and the ignored. They are not told to cheer up. Instead, Jesus urges them to draw near. "Come to me, all you who are weary and burdened, and I will give you rest." Jesus urges us in Matthew 11:28–30, "Take my yoke upon you and learn from me, for I am gentle and humble in heart, and you will find rest for your souls. For my yoke is easy and my burden is light."

Not About Us

It is common for those who lead worship to remind the congregation that worship is "not about us." This is certainly true in many respects. We do not worship ourselves. God is the object of our worship and should be at the center of the service. Worship is not entertainment. Although we may enjoy the experience, the main objective of worship is not to amuse or distract. We do not have to like the experience of worship in order for it to be true worship. Indeed, the Bible offers ample evidence which suggests that this side of eternity the experience of God's presence is often accompanied by discomfort. Those who draw near to God become aware of their sin and His holiness. They are more likely to cry "woe" than "whoopee" (Isa. 6:5; Rev. 1:17).

To say that worship is "not about us" is a reminder that God evaluates worship. God does not find all worship that is offered to Him acceptable. Some acts of worship are better than others. Some forms are illegitimate. This has been true since the very beginning. God looked with favor on Abel's sacrifice and rejected the offering of Cain (Gen. 4:4–5). Yet it is just here that we must be most careful. God does not make such distinctions based on personal preference the way we do. Abel's sacrifice was not preferred over Cain's because God had a taste for meat and Cain only offered him bread. Faith was the ingredient that made Abel's sacrifice more palatable (Heb. 11:4). It is faith in Jesus Christ and His atoning sacrifice that makes our worship acceptable.

Yet to say that worship is "not about us" may give the impression that the only thing that matters in worship is whether God likes it. This is only half true. As far as we can tell from Scripture, God does not favor one particular style of music over another. Psalm 150:3–5 mentions a diversity of instruments and modes of expression. God may be perfectly pleased with forms and expressions of worship that we would find intolerable. We, however, are not as flexible as God in this matter. Most of us prefer a particular style.

I like the music I grew up with. I hate the music my kids listen to. Of course, tastes can change. My father was a huge fan of jazz. Not the "cool jazz" of today but the old-school jazz of Bix Beiderbecke, Louis Armstrong, and Fats Waller. As a kid, I hated his music. When I became an adult, especially after my father died, I found that I liked it because it reminded me of him. But most of our musical tastes are relatively narrow, fixed within a limited range of styles. To the extent that these preferences shape our experience, worship *has* to be "about us." The less comfortable I am with the style of worship, the less likely I am to engage in worship.

Three Observations

In view of this, I want to make three practical observations. First, it is time that the church stopped trying to please everyone when it comes to worship. Given the great variety of styles and tastes in music, it is not possible to please all the people all the time. As a corollary to this, we should not feel guilty about our own dissatisfaction with some styles of worship. I think it is very possible that I would not enjoy every instrument the psalmist includes in his list, and I am certain that the particular style of music to which he was accustomed would sound alien to my ears. If this is true, we don't need to be ashamed of the fact that we really do hate some of the music we hear in church. At the same time, the psalmist's directive also means that it is unreasonable to expect everyone else to agree with my personal tastes. This is the greater challenge. It is not hard for me to come to terms with my personal dislike of your favorite style of worship. It is far more difficult for me to accept the fact that you like it.

We cannot help being profoundly affected by the music we hear. Music affects us on every level: neurologically, physiologically, aesthetically, and emotionally. When someone says to me, "I just can't worship to that music," I believe them. But the Bible's description of the worship of heaven suggests that the variety of musical styles, the type of instruments used, and the methods which the church employs in its worship should exceed the scope of my personal taste.

Second, we should admit that quality is not always the most important factor in the music that shapes our worship experience. Clearly, some music is better than other music. A Beethoven piano concerto is qualitatively better than "Chopsticks." Although it is tempting to think that we should only offer God the best quality music, personal taste makes this unrealistic. The worship that moves me most and is the most effective vehicle for helping me to enter into God's presence may not always include the "best" music. This is as true of traditional worship styles as it is of contemporary. A traditional worship style does not always guarantee that the music will be good, if by "good" we mean music that is sophisticated in its composition or accomplished in its performance. Likewise, contemporary worship does not always mean that the music will sound like a commercial jingle.

However, the emotional potential of music also greatly increases the possibility of manipulation. A church that narrowly identifies worship with a particular kind of emotional state will be tempted to use worship, and especially the music of worship, as an external stimulant to induce that state in those who are present. Emotion is an important and legitimate aspect of our Christian experience. In ordinary life, emotion is the energy that enables us to put thought into action. But it is possible for emotion to become an end in itself. When this happens, legitimate emotion deteriorates into sentimentalism.

> • • •
> *We do not all have to like the same worship style, but we do need to show respect for our differences.*
> • • •

Third, it is not our differences in musical taste that have caused the most damage to the church when it comes to worship. Rather, it is our mutual contempt and lack of respect. What has hurt us most has been our unwillingness to acknowledge that all of us have sacrificed. To some extent, everybody is disappointed with something when it comes to worship. It is not realistic for me to expect the church's worship to be tailored to my personal tastes. I must sometimes sing (or at least hear) music that does not appeal to me and listen to sermons that do not always seem suited to my life situation. We do not all have to like the same worship style, but we do need to show respect for our differences.

The ultimate antidote to our disappointment with congregational worship is humility. True humility does not abandon its preferences but knows when to set them aside. Perhaps our worship leaders were right after all. Worship is not about us. Worship is not a private practice. It is the chief work of heaven and the duty of every creature. A day will come when our conflict and mutual discomfort over the church's worship will end. Until then, we must muddle through the best we can by reminding ourselves that we are part of a much larger congregation. It is one populated by patriarchs and prophets, saints and angels, and where we are invited to join a chorus which was begun on the first day of Creation. The first notes were sounded by those who surround God's throne in heaven. Their theme echoes through the rest of His domain. All that remains is for us to add our voices to their song.

10

Happily Ever After

When Heaven Becomes a Real Place

**"He will wipe every tear from their eyes.
There will be no more death or mourning or crying or pain,
for the old order of things has passed away."**

—*REVELATION 21:4*

When we were children in Sunday school, we were taught to look forward to going to heaven. We used to sing, "Heaven is a wonderful place, filled with glory and grace."

But not everyone looks forward to heaven. My best friend in college, although he was a serious Christian, once admitted to me that he was nervous about heaven. He had been reading the New Testament book of Revelation and it seemed to him that all the saints did there was bow up and down before the throne of God. This did not sound like a very interesting activity to him. Nor did it seem like a good way to spend eternity.

My friend and Mark Twain agree. In his satirical portrait of heaven, Twain envisioned a giant but benevolent bureaucracy where newly arrived souls stand in line for a long time to be checked in. Those who take the figurative language and allegories of the

Bible literally ask for a halo and a harp and are given them. "They go and sing and play just about one day, and that's the last you'll ever see them in the choir," Twain explains. "They don't need anybody to tell them that that sort of thing wouldn't make a heaven—at least not a heaven that a sane man could stand a week and remain sane."[1]

Heaven as we have traditionally pictured it is an uninspiring place, a subject of clichés, and the butt of jokes. It is the green space where our loved ones go after they die, not unlike the cemetery itself. It is a quiet and comfortable spot from which our deceased parents and grandparents view significant events like graduations, weddings, family reunions, and presumably their own funerals. Like spectators on a hill who watch from a great distance, they "look down upon us" but cannot do much else.

If this is heaven, what makes it heavenly? Such earthly affairs are tedious enough for the living. One can only wonder what they would be like for souls who were permitted to watch but not participate. Would they find our small talk about yesterday's game or our employer's irritating behavior to be interesting? Would they enjoy knowing that we missed them? Would they be distressed at the sight of our troubles? The inhabitants of this heaven would be more like Marley's ghost than the angels. They might seek to interfere for good, but would lack the power to do so. If heaven is really only a distant gallery from which the departed observe affairs as they unfold on earth, then it is a dull place indeed. It is more like that boring relative's house your parents forced you to visit when you were a kid—the one without Nintendo or any children your own age—than the place where God's throne dwells.

The popular view of heaven pictures a realm so far removed from us that our voice will not carry to its shores. It is close enough for the departed to watch us but too far away to have any real effect on earth. This traditional view of heaven is much like our view of retirement. We believe it is real. We may even look forward to it, but only in a vague and undefined way. The reality is too removed from our present experience to sustain our interest and too far in the future to help us in the present. And we are afraid that when it finally arrives, it will be less than we had expected.

Heaven as a Mirror of Earth

For the most part, the church has always believed in heaven, but its view of heaven has been far from monolithic. The church's notions about heaven have changed with the times. Down through the ages the church has often imagined a heaven that mirrored its own values. Colleen McDannell and Bernhard Lang note that the early church fathers envisioned a heaven that reflected spiritual values like asceticism. Some, like Irenaeus, imagined heaven as a glorified material world. Others pictured it as a spiritual and ascetic realm where spirit replaced matter and family ties disappeared. Still others joined these two visions together and thought of heaven as a place of semi-spiritual existence, where the saints will dwell with perfect bodies.[2]

The expectation of the medieval church changed with the culture. According to McDannell and Lang, the medieval idea of heaven was shaped by the rise of city life, the intellectualized spirituality of medieval scholasticism, and the social structure of court life. The medieval church understood heaven to be a place much like the city state of its own day, with God enthroned as its king and surrounded by a heavenly court. Like its earthly counterpart, the social structure of heaven was divided into ranks. But unlike earth, heavenly nobility was determined by spiritual merit instead of birth. In this heaven, earthly activity was replaced by the contemplation of God and the ecstasies of mystic love.

Instead of speculating about the details of heavenly experience, the Reformers reflected on the earthly implications of Christ's bodily resurrection and ascension. Luther and Calvin differed in their view of the manner in which Christ continued to manifest His presence to the church after His ascension. Luther believed Christ's body was literally present "in, with, and under" the elements of the Lord's Supper. Although his "small catechism" states that Christ visibly ascended to heaven and entered the glory of the Father, he also asserts that Christ, according to His human nature, "rules and fills all things with divine power and majesty."[3] Luther believed that Jesus' body was omnipresent. He did not see Christ's ascension as movement across space from one location to another like someone "climbing into a house by means of a ladder," but as a visible demonstration of His exaltation and supremacy over all of creation.[4]

Calvin, on the other hand, taught that the literal body of Jesus was in heaven and not on earth. He said that Christ's power and presence, however, were "diffused and spread beyond all the bounds of heaven and earth" by means of the Holy Spirit's ministry.[5] In the *Institutes of the Christian Religion* Calvin explains: "Carried up into heaven, therefore, he withdrew his bodily presence from our sight, not to cease to be present with believers still on their earthly pilgrimage, but to rule heaven and earth with a more immediate power."[6] Those who partake of the Lord's Supper do not bring Christ down to earth; instead they are "lifted up" into His presence by "the secret working of His Spirit."[7]

In the First Great Awakening, American pastor and theologian Jonathan Edwards talked about heaven in a way that reflected his

Calvinistic Puritan heritage. He taught that admittance to heaven was a matter of grace and given as a gift to all believers through faith in Jesus Christ, but he warned that not all would be granted the same degree of reward. Edwards urged his congregation to set their expectation on the hope of heaven and reject the world with all its enjoyments. But this God-centered perspective eventually turned inward. In his survey of changing American views of heaven and the afterlife, historian Gary Scott Smith notes, "In the middle decades of the nineteenth century, Americans' vision of heaven changed dramatically, from one centered on God to one focused on humans."[8] This was a vision of heaven shaped by the ideals of Victorian middle-class family life.

. . .

Although a majority of Christians still believes that heaven exists, their primary field of interest seems to be earth.

. . .

In our day heaven has fallen on hard times. Although a majority of Christians still believes that heaven exists, their primary field of interest seems to be earth. This devaluation of heaven's real estate has happened for theological reasons. Many have taken the church to task for being too heavenly minded and not concerned enough about the earth.

New Testament scholar N. T. Wright is a good example. In his book *Surprised by Hope*, Wright argues, "Heaven, in the Bible, is not a future destiny but the other, hidden, dimension of our ordinary life—God's dimension, if you like."[9] Those who hold this view do not condemn the church for believing in heaven so much as they chide it for failing to integrate its hope of heaven with God's intent for earth.

This contemporary perspective actually follows a trajectory

begun at the end of the nineteenth century with the rise of the so-cial gospel, a view of the church's mission that argued "refashion-ing earth to mirror heaven was as important as preparing people to go to heaven."[10] Although once associated mostly with theological liberalism, this kind of social activism is now widely endorsed by theological conservatives as well.

Heaven Is a Wonderful Place

Perhaps we should not be surprised by such a diversity of views. The Beatles' John Lennon sang, "Imagine there's no heaven, it's easy if you try." While there is little in his song that agrees with what the Bible has to say about heaven, Lennon got it right on one point. It is easier to imagine that heaven *does not* exist than it is to imagine heaven *as* it exists. There are many good reasons we find it difficult to "get a handle" on heaven. For one thing, heaven is hard to put into words. It contains that which no eye has seen, no ear has heard, and no mind has conceived (see 1 Cor. 2:9). Earth is the only frame of reference we have this side of eternity. If we cannot understand heaven in terms of earth, then we cannot un-derstand it at all. It is not surprising, then, that we would try to imagine heaven in earthly terms.

What is more, there is some biblical warrant for doing so. The Bible itself often uses earthly analogies to describe heavenly reali-ties. The old clichés which characterize heaven as a place where the streets are paved with gold and the city walls are made of jew-els come from biblical descriptions of the New Jerusalem (see Rev. 21:10–21). Despite the intentional absurdity of Twain's portrait, there are good theological reasons for seeing heaven through the lens of earth.

Heaven is not the earth, but there is some continuity between the two. Jesus distinguished heaven from earth when He taught the church to pray for God's will to be done in the Lord's Prayer (Matt. 6:10). At the same time, His petition clearly acknowledges both heaven and earth as the rightful domain of God. To use the imagery of Scripture, heaven is where God's "throne" is and the Earth is His "footstool" (Ps. 123:1; Isa. 66:1). Does this mean that there is literally a chair in heaven where God sits? This may actually be true for Christ, who now resides in bodily form in heaven. But in general it seems better to understand such language as a reference to divine power and authority rather than being a description of the furniture of heaven. We certainly do not believe that Isaiah was being literal when he spoke of the earth as God's footstool. God is not floating on a cloud and resting His feet on our planet.

However, if we take the Bible's language at face value when it speaks of heaven, we must also acknowledge that the little song about heaven that we learned in Sunday school was correct on one fundamental point. Heaven is a real place. Heaven does not appear on any map. It cannot be seen from our most powerful telescopes. But it is a true location. The Bible may sometimes use metaphors and similes to describe what heaven is like, but heaven itself is not merely a figure of speech, spiritual concept, or state of mind. The Bible describes heaven as a location. God speaks "from heaven" (Gen. 21:17; 22:11, 15; Ex. 20:22; Deut. 4:36; 2 Sam. 22:14; Neh. 9:13). He also hears prayer "from heaven" which is His "dwelling place" (1 Kings 8:34, 36, 39, 42, 45, 49; Neh. 9:13). Angels come "from heaven" (Dan. 4:13, 23; Rev. 18:1). Jesus said He was the one who had "come down from heaven" to do the Father's will (John 6:38). He told Nicodemus: "No one has ever gone into heaven except the one who came from heaven—the Son of Man" (John 3:13).

The Bible's use of directional language when speaking of heaven has prompted some theologians to warn against taking these descriptions too literally. When the Bible speaks of Jesus or the angels "going up" or "coming down" from heaven, they note that we should not think that the writer is attempting to describe heaven's location in geographic terms. If God is omnipresent, He is no farther from earth than He is from heaven. "Basically, heaven and earth in biblical cosmology are not two different locations within the same continuum of space or matter," N. T. Wright explains. "They are two different dimensions of God's good creation."[11]

> . . .
> *Earth is the dominion of Christ as much as heaven, but it is a realm where we do not presently "see everything subject to Him."*
> . . .

But if heaven is not, as another Sunday school song told us, "somewhere in outer space," why does the Bible use language that sounds both directional and spatial to describe it? The answer is that such language is not meant to plot its position relative to the points on a compass (or on an altimeter). It is intended to orient heaven and earth in terms of their relationship to one another and to God.

When the Bible speaks of heaven as God's throne and the earth as His footstool, it describes earth in relation to divine authority. Heaven is the realm where divine authority reigns supreme. It is the place where the Father's "will" is always done and where His authority goes unchallenged. Earth is also the Father's domain, but because of the entrance of sin into this realm, it is a place where God's authority is challenged. It is on earth where the "kings of the earth take their stand and the rulers gather together against the Lord and against his Anointed One" (Ps. 2:2). Earth is the dominion of Christ as much as heaven, but it is a realm where we do not presently "see everything subject to him" (Heb. 2:8). Heaven, on the other hand, is the realm where Jesus is "now crowned with glory and honor" (Heb. 2:9).

Our Father in Heaven

Yet the spatial language that the Bible uses when speaking of heaven emphasizes the proximity of heaven and earth as much as it underscores the distance that exists between them. It is all too true that earth is not heaven. Nevertheless, the earth upon which we live is never beyond heaven's view. When Jesus taught us to pray to "our Father in heaven," He used a form of address that implicitly promised that we would be seen and heard by the One to whom we pray. The Father who sees all that occurs knows what is done in secret (Matt. 6:4, 6). He hears our every word, and knows what we need even before we ask (Matt. 6:8). We live constantly within His sight and are always within earshot. To use the words of theologian Helmut Thielicke, "We walk beneath an open heaven."[12]

What is more, because of Christ's victory over sin, we also live under the authority of heaven. This is the gospel of the kingdom. It is the good news that, through Christ, the Father has "rescued us from the dominion of darkness and brought us into the kingdom of the Son he loves" (Col. 1:13). We are under new management and are subject to a greater power than the power of sin that once ruled our thoughts and actions. This new state of affairs was anticipated by Christ in the second petition of the Lord's Prayer, which says: "your kingdom come, your will be done on earth as it is in heaven" (Matt. 6:10).

This petition does more than look forward to the final consummation of Christ's kingdom. It certainly does anticipate the day when Jesus is enthroned in Jerusalem and "the kingdom of the world has become the kingdom of our Lord and of his Christ" (Rev. 11:15). But like the other petitions of the Lord's Prayer, it also asks the Father to act in the present. The request for God's will to be done on earth as it is in heaven has as much immediate significance as the petitions for daily bread, forgiveness, protection from temptation, and deliverance from evil. All these will find their ultimate fulfillment when Christ reigns supreme. Our experience in the present is merely an advance on that account. But these petitions also indicate that we live in a world that is intersected by the overlapping domain of heaven. Theologian Thomas F. Torrance has described the relationship between these two realms as being like that of two hemispheres which intersect "so that there is an area in which the content of one belongs to the content of another."[13]

Yet despite Jesus' encouragement to pray these words, the kingdom does not seem to "stick." It is all too apparent that the earth is not magically transformed into heaven because we utter these words. We see proof of this every night on the television news or read about it on the Internet. Nation rises against nation as famines, pestilences, and earthquakes stalk their inhabitants. Jesus warned that these were merely "the beginning of birth pains" (Matt. 24:8; Mark 13:8). Beyond these great events are all the little tidal waves that wash over our personal lives and scatter our hopes. Our marriage falters. The doctor diagnoses us with cancer. The child we nurtured to adulthood treats us like a stranger. We lose our job. We agonize over our continuing personal struggle with sin.

Experiences like these serve as blunt reminders that, for now, we inhabit these two realms simultaneously. On the one hand, we must live in a world that continues to be scarred by the collateral damage of sin. It is a world that "groans" as it waits for liberation from its bondage to decay (Rom. 8:21–22). On the other hand, the Scriptures also assure us that we have been mysteriously moved into the kingdom of the Father's beloved Son (Col. 1:13). We live "on earth" but we are also seated in the heavenly realms by virtue of being "in Christ Jesus" (Eph. 2:6).

In other words, we live at the intersection of two distinct but related kingdoms. One is a kingdom of entropy and the other of eternity. One is perpetually winding down and in a state of decay. The other is continually renewed. One is a kingdom of dusk and growing darkness. The other is a kingdom of approaching dawn and eternal light.

On this side of Christ's return we must live at the point of tension between these two realms, proclaiming the gospel of grace and announcing the approach of Christ and His kingdom. This mission involves both action and waiting. As we act on Christ's behalf, we announce the good news of forgiveness through Christ and pray for Him to reveal the reality of His dominion in our daily experience. These prayers,

. . .

Redemption is not merely rehabilitation. Jesus meant it when He told Pilate that His kingdom was not of this world.

. . .

combined with our own Spirit-empowered effort, create points of entry where our experience on earth correlates with the order of heaven. God's will is done in us and around us. But this good effort does not and cannot fundamentally change the nature of the fallen world. We are not trying to draw heaven down to earth by sheer effort. Nor are we attempting to renovate the earth and turn it into heaven.

Redemption is not merely rehabilitation. Jesus meant it when

He told Pilate that His kingdom was not of this world (John 18:36). The world as we know it is passing away and will one day dissolve in fire and heat (1 John 2:17; 2 Pet. 3:10-12). We are waiting for a new heavens and a new earth (2 Pet. 3:13).

Happy Ending

Here, then, is the happy ending to our story and the ultimate remedy for our disappointment. The Bible promises that one day the division between heaven and earth will finally be removed. The result will not be the elimination of one or the other but a marriage between the two. The book of Revelation pictures a day when heaven and earth will be made new and the city of God will descend from heaven "prepared as a bride beautifully dressed for her husband" (Rev. 21:1–2).

In this new creation, the old distinction between heaven and earth will no longer be meaningful. Earth will be the dwelling place of God as much as heaven. Intimacy with God, which was previously only symbolized in the tabernacle and later embodied in the incarnation of our Savior, will be experienced by all who dwell there. God will be "with us" and will wipe away every tear from our eyes (Rev. 21:3). What will this experience be like? The information which the Bible provides is not specific enough to paint a picture in detail—though, as we have already seen, this has not stopped the church from trying. Speculation about the architectural details of the "mansions" or how we will employ ourselves on a daily basis in eternity is mere conjecture. Yet we do know some things.

We know that our experience will be an embodied one (Job 19:26; 1 Cor. 15:42–49; Phil. 3:21; 1 John 3:2). We will not float about eternity like ghosts. Our experience will also be personal and relational. We will not lose our identity or be absorbed into a divine "Other," but each of us will continue to possess our individual consciousness and soul. If the scenes described in the early chapters of the book of Revelation are any indication, we will recall our past experience and will worship in community with other believers (Rev. 6:9–10; 7:9–10).

Out of the ashes of the old world a new and better paradise will be created. It will have some of the features of the old. For example, the Tree of Life will be there (Rev. 2:7; 22:2, 14). But there will also be significant differences. There will no longer be any night. The light of the sun will not be necessary in this new world. God's servants will reign forever (Rev. 22:5). Our relationships will continue, but they will change since there will no longer be any marriage but rather a state of being more "like the angels in heaven" (Matt. 22:30).

Beyond this, relatively little is known. We can guess, perhaps, but we cannot know for certain what our experience will be like. However, if heavenly experience surpasses earthly, as Jesus implied in His remark to Nicodemus in John 3:3, then we can be certain that it will be far better than anything we can hope or dream. If "our present sufferings are not worth comparing with the glory that will be revealed in us," then neither are our present joys or pleasures (Rom. 8:18).

Hell Is for Real

It would be cruel to conclude this reflection without acknowledging that the Bible speaks of a third realm and another more terrible destiny prepared for those who refuse the grace of God. If it is true that "heaven is for real," then we must also acknowledge that hell is a real place too. Those who accept the Bible as their ultimate authority on eternal matters cannot have one without the other. Furthermore, much of what has been said about heaven can also be asserted about hell. It is a real place. It is described in biblical language that may point to realties that are beyond our earthly experience. Hell is not the final destination of the damned. In the end, death and hell will be cast into the "lake of fire." This is what the Bible calls "the second death" and will be the fate of all who are not in Christ (Rev. 20:14–15).

In this age that teaches its children that everyone who competes deserves a trophy, the idea of "hell" has also fallen on hard times. In this spiritual landscape in which the real estate of heaven has been seriously devalued, hell has all but disappeared. Yet Jesus affirmed hell's existence and warned about it (Matt. 5:22; 29, 30; 10:28; 18:9; 23:33; Mark 9:43, 45, 47; Luke 12:5; 16:23). Like heaven, theologians disagree about how literally we should take the Bible's language about hell. The Scriptures sometimes describe the experience of the lost souls in eternity in terms that seem to us to be mutually exclusive. It is a place of flames but also of "outer darkness" (Matt. 8:12; 22:13; 25:30). What is clear, however, is that the sufferings the Bible describes are those of a personal, conscious torment that lasts forever (Mark 9:43, 48; Luke 16:23).

The church has tried to use hell as a spiritual stick meant to motivate us to do right and shun wrong. This approach has not been very effective.

Popular literature sometimes pictures hell as the devil's heaven, a place where Satan rules and the demons wreak havoc on the souls of the damned. But the Bible portrays it differently. Hell is the dominion of God as much as heaven is. However, hell differs from heaven in that it is a domain of unmitigated justice. There is no grace in hell. Hell will be the destiny of those who have chosen not to experience the grace and forgiveness that comes through Jesus Christ and His suffering. It will not be a place where departed sinners party together for eternity. The inhabitants of hell will experience regret and unfulfilled longing forevermore.

Down through the centuries, the church has tried to use hell as a spiritual stick meant to motivate us to do right and shun wrong. It must be admitted that this approach has not been very effective. The church's traditional teaching about hell has not curbed human sinfulness. What is more, contemporary discomfort with the idea of eternal punishment has turned hell into an empty threat. Modern worshipers find it hard to imagine God casting anyone into hell, let alone consigning them to a lake of fire. Theirs is a God who is all mercy and no justice, one whose bark is worse than His bite. Like an irascible but kindly old grandpa, He speaks gruffly to sinners but will relent in the end with a wink. It is hard to imagine such a God sending His Son to suffer in our place. Why would there be any need to do so?

To me the most convincing evidence for the reality of hell is the suffering of Christ on the cross. That suffering is also, perhaps, our best glimpse into the nature of hell. Jesus' cry over God's abandonment at the cross captures the essence of hell's greatest torment (Matt. 27:46; Mark 15:34).

We should not think of hell as a space where God is not. If He is truly omnipresent, then He is as present in hell as He is anywhere else. But the inhabitants of hell are those who have been "shut out from the presence" of God's majesty and power (2 Thess. 1:9). One of the greatest torments of hell must be the awareness that the God of glory is as infinitely inaccessible as He is immeasurably near. Imagine the burning desire of your deepest unfulfilled longing combined with the shame of rejection. If you multiply that exponentially, you will only have begun to grasp what it will be like to experience final condemnation.

The Great Divorce

The church's teaching about heaven and hell has prompted some to ask a troubling question: Can there even be a heaven if there is a hell? We cannot imagine enjoying the delights of a new heaven and earth as long as we are aware that there are souls who are tormented in hell or the lake of fire. It is this dilemma more than any other that has caused some today to reject the doctrine of hell. But the view from the new heaven and earth is different from the view from here.

In his book *The Great Divorce*, C. S. Lewis imagines a dream in which his main character, presumably Lewis himself, takes a bus trip from hell to heaven. During this visit he comes upon George MacDonald, the Scottish fantasy writer and preacher whose writings first attracted Lewis to Christ. During their encounter, MacDonald explains to Lewis that heaven and hell work backward. "Not only this valley but all this earthly past will have been Heaven to those who are saved," MacDonald explains. "Not only the twilight in that town, but all their life on earth too, will be seen by the damned to have been Hell."[14]

> *Those who belong to Christ are not merely transported into the kingdom, we are changed by it.*

This exchange mirrors a point made by Lewis himself in the preface of the book, when he writes that in the end earth will not be found to be a very distinctive place by anyone: "I think earth, if chosen instead of heaven, will turn out to have been all along, only a region in Hell: and earth, if put second to Heaven, to have been from the beginning a part of Heaven itself."[15]

Can there ever be a heaven for us while we know that there is a hell? Not as long as we remain as we are. But for those who belong to Christ, the power of the kingdom is the power to reach back and draw all things into itself. We are not merely transported into God's kingdom, we are changed by it. The same power that causes "all things" to work for the good of those who have been called according to God's purpose, also works to conform us into the image of His Son (Rom. 8:28–30).

When His work is complete, we will see things as God sees them. In that day, all disappointment and grief will be forgotten. We will love what God loves and hate what He hates. Every tear will be dried and all regret abandoned. Amen. Even so, come, Lord Jesus.

Acknowledgments

I am very grateful to Dave DeWit and Paul Santhouse for their friendship, encouragement, and affirmation, which motivated me to embark on this project. My thanks also goes to Duane Sherman, Barnabas Piper, and Johannah Hensler for enabling it to see the light of day and find an audience. I must also express appreciation to Mark Galli (at *Christianity Today*) and Brian Larson (formerly of *PreachingToday.com*) for their interest in my work. Several of the chapters in this book were developed out of articles that first appeared in their publications.

It has always been my privilege to work with excellent editors and this project is no exception. It has been a pleasure to work with Ed Gilbreath, whose skill as a writer makes him a joy to work with as an editor.

My love and appreciation are due to my wife, Jane, who always serves as my first editor, most affectionate critic, and greatest fan. I also want to thank my agent, Mark Sweeney, for his effort and enthusiasm on my behalf. Most of all, I am indebted to my Lord Jesus Christ. Those who put their trust in Him will never be put to shame (Rom. 9:33).

Notes

Chapter 1: False Hope and Unreasonable Expectations

1. Jean Kilbourne, "Jesus Is a Pair of Jeans," *New Internationalist*, September 2006, 10–12.

2. Joseph R. Myers, *The Search to Belong: Rethinking Intimacy, Community and Small Groups* (Grand Rapids: Zondervan, 2003), 50.

3. Ibid., 51.

4. I am indebted to my friend and former student Michael Reed, who coined this phrase, for sparking my thinking about this.

5. C. S. Lewis, *The Problem of Pain* (New York: HarperCollins, 1966), 33.

6. Ibid.

7. Alexander MacLaren, *The Gospel of St. Matthew*, vol. 1 (London: Hodder & Stoughton, 1892), 202.

8. Anthony Bloom, *Beginning to Pray* (New York: Paulist, 1970), 26.

9. Ibid.

10. Helmut Thielicke, *The Prayer that Spans the World: Sermons on the Lord's Prayer*, trans. James Doberstein (Cambridge, England: James Clark, 1978), 59.

11. Ibid., 60.

Chapter 2: As Good as His Word

1. According to the Masoretic text, the phrase in verse 22 should read "the Lord remained standing before Abraham."

2. C. S. Lewis, *The World's Last Night and Other Essays* (San Diego: Houghton Mifflin Harcourt, 1960), 5.

3. Ibid., 10–11.

Chapter 3: Jesus Disappoints Everyone

1. N. T. Wright, *Surprised by Hope: Rethinking Resurrection, Heaven and the Mission of the Church* (New York: HarperCollins, 2008), 5.

2. C. S. Lewis, *The Weight of Glory* (New York: HarperOne, 1976), 26.

3. C. S. Lewis, *Mere Christianity* (New York: HarperCollins, 1980), 3.

Chapter 4: The Awkward Conversation of Prayer

1. Helmut Thielicke, *Encounter With Spurgeon* (Grand Rapids: Baker, 1963), 10.

2. Eugene Peterson, *Working the Angles: The Shape of Pastoral Integrity* (Grand Rapids: Eerdmans, 1987), 44.

3. Harry Emerson Fosdick, *The Meaning of Prayer* (New York: Association Press, 1917), 149. Italics are the author's.

4. Martyn Lloyd-Jones, *Spiritual Depression: Its Causes and Its Cure* (Grand Rapids: Eerdmans, 1965), 21.

5. J. C. Ryle, *Home Truths: Being Miscellaneous Tracts and Addresses* (London: William Hunt, 1887), 130.

Chapter 5: Asleep at the Wheel

1. Harry Emerson Fosdick, *The Meaning of Prayer* (New York: Association Press, 1917), 64.

2. Helmut Thielicke, *Christ and the Meaning of Life* (Cambridge: James Clarke & Co., 1965), 13.

3. Alain de Boton, *Status Anxiety* (New York: Vintage, 2004), 27.

4. Karen Lee-Thorp, "Is Beauty the Beast?" *Christianity Today*, July 14, 1997, 30.

5. Henry Drummond, *Addresses* (Philadelphia: Henry Alttemus, 1891), 110.

Chapter 6: Great Expectations or Delusions of Grandeur?

1. G. K. Chesterton, *Tremendous Trifles* (New York: Dodd, Mead & Co., 1920), 7.

2. Stanley Hauerwas, *Vision and Virtue: Essays in Christian Ethical Reflection* (South Bend, IN: Univ. of Notre Dame, 1981), 46.

3. Ibid., 47.

4. Ibid., 46.

Chapter 7: Eat, Drink, and Be Hungry

1. Joachim Jeremias, *New Testament Theology* (New York: Scribners, 1971), 289–90.

2. Ibid., 290.

3. Joachim Jeremias, *The Prayers of Jesus* (Philadelphia: Fortress, 1984), 100.

4. John Noland, *The Gospel of Matthew: A Commentary on the Greek Text* (Grand Rapids: Eerdmans, 2005), 290.

5. Helmut Thielicke, *The Prayer That Spans the World*, trans. John W. Doberstein (Cambridge: James Clarke, 1965), 81.

6. Alexander MacLaren, *The Gospel of St. Matthew*, vol. 1 (London: Hodder & Stoughton, 1892), 95–96.

Chapter 8: Take This Job

1. Eugene Peterson, *Leap Over a Wall: Earthy Spirituality for Everyday Christians* (San Francisco: Harper, 1997), 31.

2. The two standards emphasized in Colossians 4:1 are what is "right" and what is "fair." Compensation is to be "in proportion to the service rendered." See John Murray, *Principles of Conduct: Aspects of Biblical Ethics* (Grand Rapids: Eerdmans, 1957), 99.

3. According to Matthew 25:14, Jesus begins the parable with the introductory phrase: "Again, it will be like . . ." This indicates that the parable is a continuation of the theme reflected in the opening phrase of Matthew 25:1 ("At that time the kingdom of heaven will be like . . .") and prompted by the question of the disciples in Matthew 24:3 about the nature of Christ's return. This is further confirmed by Luke 19:11.

4. Some may feel that Paul's directives to slaves have no relevance for the workplace. John Murray argues convincingly that they do: "The implications of obedience for the freeman are no less significant. We must not become so absorbed in the questions that pertain to slavery that we discount, or overlook, the demand for obedience as it applies to the free. That Paul, for example, has the free in view as well as the bond is apparent from Ephesians 6:8 (cf. 1 Corinthians 7:21, 22)." *Principles of Conduct: Aspects of Biblical Ethics* (Grand Rapids: Eerdmans, 1957), 103.

5. Ibid.

6. Ibid., 104.

7. Max DePree, *Leadership Is an Art* (New York: Doubleday, 2004), 21.

Chapter 9: The Trajectory of Worship

1. Eugene Peterson, *Working the Angles: The Shape of Pastoral Integrity* (Grand Rapids: Eerdmans, 1987), 47.

2. The quote comes from a sermon by Jonathan Edwards entitled "Praise, One of the Chief Employments of Heaven" that he preached on November 7, 1734. Among other places it can be found in *Classic Sermons of Praise*, comp. Warren W. Wiersbe (Grand Rapids: Kregel, 1994), 45–63.

3. Jeremy Begbie, *Resounding Truth: Christian Wisdom in the World of Music* (Grand Rapids: Baker, 2007), 57.

4. Ibid.

5. Ibid., 294.

6. Ibid., 36.

Chapter 10: Happily Ever After

1. Mark Twain, *Extract from Captain Stormfield's Visit to Heaven* (New York: Harper, 1909), 40.

2. Colleen McDannell and Bernhard Lang, *Heaven: A History* (New Haven, CT: Yale Univ. Press, 1988), 67.

3. Martin Luther, *Luther's Small Catechism* (St. Louis: Concordia, 1943), 118–19. See questions 153 & 154.

4. Werner Elert, *The Structure of Lutheranism*, Walter A. Hansen, trans. (St. Louis: Concordia, 1962), 252.

5. John Calvin, *Institutes of the Christian Religion*, *2.16.14*, John T. McNeill, ed., Ford Lewis Battles, trans., vol. 1 (Philadelphia: Westminster), 523.

6. Ibid.

7. Ibid., 4.17.31, 1403.

8. Gary Scott Smith, *Heaven in the American Imagination* (New York: Oxford, 2011), 71.

9. N. T. Wright, *Surprised by Hope: Rethinking Heaven, the Resurrection, and the Mission of the Church* (New York: HarperOne, 2008), 18.

10. Smith, *Heaven in the American Imagination* (New York: Oxford, 2011), 135.

11. Wright, *Surprised by Hope* (New York: HarperOne, 2008), 111.

12. Helmut Thielicke, *Life Can Begin Again* (Philadelphia: Fortress, 1963), 22.

13. Thomas F. Torrance, *Preaching Christ Today* (Grand Rapids: Eerdmans, 1994), 52.

14. C. S. Lewis, *The Great Divorce* (New York: MacMillan, 1946), 67.

15. Ibid., 7.

also available as an ebook

TRUE DISCIPLESHIP

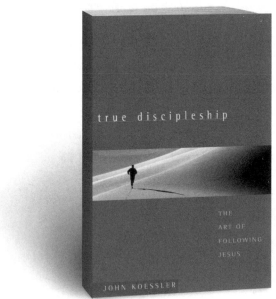

978-0-8024-1642-1

In *True Discipleship*, John Koessler provides a straightforward presentation of the characteristics Jesus required His disciples to possess. As he offers teaching on the practice and responsibility of being a disciple, readers will be stretched in their thinking and encouraged in their journey.

also available as an ebook

MOODY
PUBLISHERS
www.MoodyPublishers.com